D0072559

# Teaching PE/Health and Wellness to Elementary Teachers

*Third Edition*

Revised Printing

## Carol Girdler
*University of Iowa*

**Kendall Hunt**
publishing company

Cover photograph © 2013 Shutterstock Inc.

www.kendallhunt.com
*Send all inquiries to:*
4050 Westmark Drive
Dubuque, IA 52004-1840

Copyright © 2010, 2013, 2015 by Kendall Hunt Publishing Company

ISBN 978-1-4652-8908-7

All rights reserved. No part of this publication may be reproduced,
stored in a retrieval system, or transmitted, in any form or by any means,
electronic, mechanical, photocopying, recording, or otherwise,
without the prior written permission of the copyright owner.

Printed in the United States of America

# Contents

# Introduction

The following materials are designed to provide you, the elementary classroom teacher, with an understanding of and ideas for teaching physical education and health. My goals are for you to gain a better appreciation for both health and physical education as content areas and to leave at the end of the semester with confidence about teaching either or both subjects.

# Youth and Physical Activity: The Role of Schools

Being physically active is one of the most important steps to being healthy, and schools are an ideal setting for teaching youth how to maintain a healthy, active lifestyle. However, a study conducted in 2013 found that 44% of schools have cut back on the amount of time allotted for physical education and recess and it is estimated that only half of America's youth meet the current U.S. Health and Human Services Department evidence-based daily guideline of at least 60 minutes of moderate or vigorous intensity physical activity (Patterson, 2013). A 2006 study by the Centers for Disease Control found that only 11% of states and 57% of school districts required elementary schools to provide regularly scheduled recess (Jarrett & Waite-Stupiansky (2009). The Centers has also reported that "over the past three decades the childhood obesity rate has more than doubled for preschool children (ages 2–5) and adolescents (ages 12–19) and has more than tripled for children ages 6–11 (Kelso, n.d.)."

The opportunity for physical activity at school does not only improve the strength, flexibility, and cardiovascular health of students but also increases a students' physical competence, health-related fitness, and self-responsibility which leads to physically active individuals for a lifetime (Kelso, n.d.). Additionally, research shows that physical activity can help students focus better in class, perform better on tests, and behave better at school (Falini, 2013). According to the National Association for Sport and Physical Education, the development of physical skills learned through physical education classes can also increase self-discipline, improve judgment and goal setting abilities, and increase self-esteem (Mooney, 2014). Finally, physical education can help to strengthen peer relationships within a class and a school. Students learn to take turns, solve problems, resolve conflicts, follow rules, and work as a team.

Physically, cognitively, and emotionally, students who enjoy physical activity at school are healthier, happier, and more likely to do better cognitively. Physical activity is critical to the development of well-rounded, productive adults.

## References

Falini, L. (2013) How does recess and gym help learning at school? *Philly.com.* http://www.philly.com/philly/blogs/healthy l <ids/How-does-recess-and-gym-helplearning-at-school.html (accessed Apr 21, 2015).

Jarrett, O. & Waite-Stupiansky, S. (2009) Recess—It's Indispensable! *National Association for the Education of Young Children.* http://www.naeyc.org/files/yc/file/200909/0n%200ur%20Minds%20909.pdf (accessed Apr 21, 2015).

Kelso, C. (n.d.) The importance of physical education. *Virginia Education Association.* http://www.veanea.org/home/1000.htm (accessed Apr 21, 2015).

Mooney, L. (2014) Why is gym class important? *LIVESTRONG.COM.* http://livestrong.com/article/443955-why-is-gym-class-important/ (accessed Apr 21, 2015).

Patterson, J. (2013) Many schools cutting back on physical education. *Las Vegas Review Journal.* http://www.reviewjournal.com/news/education/many-schools-cutting-back-physical-education (accessed May 01, 2015).

## How Does Physical Activity Help?
- Builds strong bones and muscles.[1]
- Decreases the likelihood of developing obesity and risk factors for diseases like type 2 diabetes and heart disease.[1]
- May reduce anxiety and depression and promote positive mental health.[1]

## How Much Physical Activity Do Youth Need?
- **Children and adolescents should do 60 minutes (1 hour) or more of physical activity daily**[2]
  - *Aerobic Activities:* Most of the 60 or more minutes per day should be either moderate- or vigorous-intensity aerobic physical activity. Vigorous-intensity physical activity should be included at least 3 days per week.
    - Examples of aerobic activities include bike riding, walking, running, dancing, and playing active games like tag, soccer, and basketball.
  - *Muscle-strengthening Activities*: Include muscle-strengthening physical activity on at least 3 days of the week as part of the 60 or more minutes.
    - Examples of muscle-strengthening activities for younger children include gymnastics, playing on a jungle gym, and climbing a tree.
    - Examples of muscle-strengthening activities for adolescents include push-ups, pull-ups, and weightlifting exercises.

- *Bone-strengthening Activities:* Include bone-strengthening physical activity on at least 3 days of the week as part of the 60 or more minutes.
  - Examples of bone-strengthening activities include hopping, skipping, jumping, running, and sports like gymnastics, basketball, and tennis.
- Some activities may address more than one category at a time. For example, gymnastics is both muscle-strengthening and bone-strengthening while running is aerobic and bone-strengthening.
- Activities should be age-appropriate, enjoyable, and offer variety.[2]

### How Does Physical Activity Affect Academic Achievement?
- Physical activity can help youth improve their concentration, memory, and classroom behavior.[7]
- Youth who spend more time in physical education class do not have lower test scores than youth who spend less time in physical education class.[8]
- Elementary school girls who participated in more physical education had better math and reading tests scores than girls who had less time in physical education.[9]

### What Can Schools Do To Promote Physical Activity for Youth?
- Have policies that provide time for organized physical activity and free play.
- Provide information to parents about the benefits of physical activity in messages sent home and at school events.
- Encourage staff to be active. School staff and school leadership are role models for students.
- Encourage families and local groups to be involved in school-based physical activities and events.

### How Can Schools Help Youth Be More Physically Active?
A large percentage of youth physical activity can be provided through a comprehensive school-based physical activity program with quality physical education as the cornerstone. All of the parts of a physical activity program (listed below) help youth explore different physical activities and give them the chance to learn and practice the skills to establish physically active lifestyles. A comprehensive physical activity program includes the following:

### Quality Physical Education
- Gives students the knowledge and skills to participate in a lifetime of physical activity.
- Teaches movement skills and how to assess physical activity.
- Uses materials that are appropriate for the age and skill level of the students.
- Uses activities that keep students active for most of class time (more than 50% of class time).
- Meets the needs of all students.
- Is an enjoyable experience for all students.

**Policy Recommendation:** Schools should require daily physical education for students in kindergarten through grade 12 (150 minutes per week for elementary schools and 225 minutes per week for secondary schools).[10]

### Recess
- Gives students the chance to have unstructured physical activity and to practice what they learn in physical education class.
- Helps youth learn how to play together and handle conflict.[11–12]
- Improves attention and concentration in the classroom.[13–14]

**Policy Recommendation**: Schools should incorporate at least 20 minutes of recess per day in addition to physical education classes.[15]

### Physical Activity Breaks
- Build activity into classroom lessons.
- Enhance on-task classroom behavior of students.[16]

**Physical Activity Break Ideas:** Take a walk outside as part of a science class or ask students to name and act out action words from a story through physical activity.[16]

### Intramural Sports
- Offer physical activity opportunities before, during or after school hours.
- Provide students with a choice of activities like walking, running, hiking, swimming, tennis, dancing, and bicycling.
- Offer students of all skill levels an equal chance to participate.

### Interscholastic Sports
- Help students work together and engage in friendly competition.[17]
- Help students learn sport-specific and general motor skills.[17]
- May improve mental health and reduce some risky health behaviors such as cigarette smoking, illegal drug use, and having sexual intercourse.[18–19]

## Walk- and Bike-to-School Programs

- Can increase student levels of physical activity.[20]
- Promote partnerships among students, parents, and community organizations and members.
- Improve the safety of those walking and biking around schools.
- Decrease traffic near schools.

**Activity Recommendation:** Schools should participate in International Walk to School Week and support ongoing walk and bike to school programs (e.g., create safer routes to school, provide access to secure bike racks).

## How Can Schools Partner with Families and Community Groups?

- Let families know about physical activity programs at school and in the community. To make sure everyone receives the information, use different formats such as flyers, newsletters, telephone calls, e-mails, conversations at school, Internet, and media coverage.
- Include families and community members on the school health advisory council.
- Offer chances for families to participate in physical activity programs. This could include family homework assignments, activity newsletters, or family nights.
- Provide physical activity programs or workshops to students, families, and school staff. Schools can work with community organizations to allow public use of school gyms and playing fields after school hours and on weekends. Local businesses, community groups and health organizations may e able to sponsor or fund physical activity programs and events.
- Programs and messages should reflect the culture of the community and the local physical activity opportunities.

## Where Can I Find Additional Information about School-Based Physical Activity?

- U.S. Department of Health and Human Services. 2008 Physical Activity Guidelines for Americans. Washington, DC: U.S. Department of Health and Human Services; 2008. Available at: http://www.health.gov/paguidelines.
- Centers for Disease Control and Prevention. Healthy Youth! Physical Activity. Available at: http://www.cdc.gov/HealthyYouth/physicalactivity/.
- Centers for Disease Control and Prevention. Division of Nutrition, Physical Activity, and Obesity. Available at: http://www.cdc.gov/physicalactivity.
- Centers for Disease Control and Prevention. Physical Education Curriculum Analysis Tool. Atlanta, GA: U.S. Department of Health and Human Services; 2006. Available at: http://www.cdc.gov/HealthyYouth/PECAT/index.htm.
- Centers for Disease Control and Prevention. Kids Walk-to-School: A Guide to Promote Walking to School. Available at: http://www.cdc.gov/nccdphp/dnpa/kidswalk.
- National Association for Sports and Physical Activity. Comprehensive School Physical Activity Programs Package. Available at: http://iweb.aahperd.org/naspe/pdf_files/CSPAP_Package.pdf.
- National Association for Sports and Physical Activity. Integrating physical activity into the complete school day. Available at: http://www.aahperd.org/Naspe/pdf_files/integratingPA.pdf.
- The President's Council on Physical Fitness and Sports. President's Challenge Presidential Champions Program. Available at: http://www.presidentschallenge.org/index.aspx.

## References

1. U.S. Department of Health and Human Services. Physical activity guidelines advisory committee report. Washington, DC: U.S. Department of Health and Human Services; 2008.
2. U.S. Department of Health and Human Services. 2008 Physical activity guidelines for Americans. Washington, DC: U.S. Department of Health and Human Services; 2008
3. Centers for Disease Control and Prevention's National Youth Risk Behavior Surveillance—United States, 2007. Unpublished data.
4. Centers for Disease Control and Prevention. Youth Media Campaign Longitudinal Survey, 2002. *MMWR* 2003;52(33): 785–8.
5. Centers for Disease Control and Prevention. Youth Risk Behavior Surveillance—United States, 2007. *MMWR.* 2008;57(No.SS-4): 1–131.
6. McDonald MC. Active transport to school: trends among U.S. schoolchildren, 1969–2001. *American Journal of Preventive Medicine* 2007;32(6): 509–16.
7. Strong WB, Malina RM, Blimkie CJ, Daniels SR, Dishman RK, Gutin B, et al. Evidence-based physical activity for school-aged youth. *Journal of Pediatrics* 2005;146(6): 732–7.
8. Sallis JF, McKenzie TL, Kolody B, Lewis M, Marshall S, Rosengard P. Effects of health-related physical education on academic achievement: Project SPARK. *Research Quarterly for Exercise and Sport* 1999;70(2): 127–34.

9. Carlson SA, Fulton JE, Lee SM, Maynard LM, Brown DR, Kohl HW, et al. Physical education and academic achievement in elementary school: data from the early childhood longitudinal study. *American Journal of Public Health* 2008;98(4): 721–7.

10. National Association for Sport and Physical Education. Moving into the future: national standards for physical education, 2nd ed. Reston, VA: National Association for Sport and Physical Education; 2004.

11. Burdette HL, Whitaker RC. Resurrecting free play in young children: looking beyond fitness and fatness to attention, affiliation, and affect. *Archives of Pediatrics and Adolescent Medicine* 2005;159(1): 46–50.

12. Jarrett OS, Maxwell DM, Dickerson C, Hoge P, Davies G, Yetley A. Impact of recess on classroom behavior: group effects and individual differences. *Journal of Educational Research* 1998;92: 121–6.

13. Pellegrini AD, Davis PD. Relations between children's playground and classroom behaviors. *British Journal of Educational Psychology* 1993;63(Pt 1):-88–95.

14. Sluckin A. *Growing up in the playground: the social development of children.* London: Routledge & Kegan Paul; 1981.

15. National Association for Sport and Physical Education. Recess in elementary schools. Reston, VA: National Association for Sport and Physical Education; 2006.

16. Mahar MT, Murphy SK, Rowe DA, Golden J, Shields A, Raedeke TD. Effects of a classroom-based program on physical activity and on-task behavior. *Medicine and Science in Sports and Exercise* 2006;38(12): 2086–94.

17. National Association for Sport and Physical Education. Eight domains of coaching competencies. Reston, VA: National Association for Sport and Physical Education; 2006.

18. Pate RR, Trost ST, Levin S, Dowda M. Sports participation and health-related behaviors among US youth. *Archives of Pediatrics and Adolescent Medicine* 2000;154(9): 904–11.

19. Seefeldt V, Ewing ME. Youth Sports in America. *The President's Council on Physical Fitness and Sports Research Digest* 1997;2: 1–12.

20. Cooper AR. Physical activity levels of children who walk, cycle, or are driven to school. *American Journal of Preventive Medicine* 2005;29: 179–84.

# Fact Sheet for Health Professionals on Physical Activity Guidelines for Children and Adolescents

NUTRITION
PHYSICAL ACTIVITY
OBESITY

## How much physical activity do youth need?

The physical activity guidelines for children and adolescents aged 6 to 17 focuses on three types of activity: aerobic, muscle-strengthening, and bone-strengthening. Each type has important health benefits.

---

### Aerobic, Muscle-strengthening, and Bone-strengthening Activities

**Every day** children and adolescents should do **1 hour or more** of physical activity.

**Aerobic activities**. Most of the 1 hour a day should be either moderate or vigorous-intensity* aerobic physical activity, and include and include **vigorous-intensity** physical activity **at least 3 days a week**.

As a part of the 1 hour a day of physical activity, the following should be included:

- **Muscle-strengthening** on **at least 3 days a week**. These activities make muscles do more work than usual during daily life. They should involve a moderate to high level of effort and work the major muscle groups of the body: legs, hips, back, abdomen, chest, shoulders, and arms.

- **Bone-strengthening** on **at least 3 days of the week**. These activities produce a force on the bones that promotes bone growth and strength through impact with the ground.

Youth should be encouraged to engage in physical activities that are **appropriate** for their age, **enjoyable**, and offer **variety**.

No period of activity is too short to count toward the Guidelines.

---

***Intensity** is the level of effort required to do an activity.

A person doing **moderate-intensity** aerobic activity can talk, but not sing, during the activity.

A person doing **vigorous-intensity** activity cannot say more than a few words without pausing for a breath.

**U.S. DEPARTMENT OF HEALTH AND HUMAN SERVICES**
Centers for Disease Control and Prevention
Division of Nutrition, Physical Activity, and Obesity
Physical Activity Guidelines for Adults • 06/09

SAFER·HEALTHIER·PEOPLE™

# How much physical activity do youth need for health benefits?

Participating in regular physical activity provides several health benefits for youth as summarized below. Reducing risk of some of these conditions may require longer periods of participation in regular physical activity. Other benefits, such as increased heart and lung—or cardiorespiratory—fitness, may require only a few weeks or months of participation.

## Aerobic Activities

- Improved:
  - o Cardiorespiratory (aerobic) fitness and muscular strength
  - o Bone health
  - o Cardiovascular and metabolic health biomarkers
- Favorable body composition (percentages of muscle, bone, and fat)

### Moderate Evidence for Health Benefits

- Reduced symptoms of depression

# Aerobic Activities by Level of Intensity

Youth should not do only moderate-intensity activity. Including vigorous-intensity activities is important because they cause more improvement in cardiorespiratory fitness.

The intensity of aerobic physical activity can be defined on either an absolute or a relative scale. Either scale can be used to monitor the intensity of aerobic physical activity.

- **Absolute intensity** is based on the rate of energy expended during the activity, without considering cardiorespiratory fitness.
- **Relative intensity** uses cardiorespiratory fitness to assess level of effort.

Those doing moderate-intensity activity will notice their heart beating faster than normal and they will be breathing harder than normal. Those doing vigorous-intensity activity will feel their heart beating much faster and their breathing being much harder than normal.

Young people can meet the guidelines in many ways. Examples of different types of activities are included below.

## Examples of Moderate- and Vigorous-Intensity Aerobic, Muscle-Strengthening, and Bone-Strengthening Activities for Youth

| Type of Physical Activity | Children | Adolescents |
|---|---|---|
| Aerobic<br><br>Moderate–Intensity | • Active recreation such as hiking, skateboarding, rollerblading<br>• Bicycle riding*<br>• Brisk walking | • Active recreation, such as canoeing, hiking, cross-country skiing, skateboarding, rollerblading<br>• Brisk walking<br>• Bicycle riding* (stationary or road bike)<br>• Housework and yard work such as sweeping or pushing a lawn mower<br>• Playing games that require catching and throwing, such as baseball, softball |

| | | |
|---|---|---|
| **Vigorous–Intensity** | • Active games involving running and chasing, such as tag<br>• Bicycle riding*<br>• Jumping rope<br>• Martial arts, such as karate<br>• Running<br>• Sports such as ice or field hockey, basketball, swimming, tennis or gymnastics<br>• Cross-country skiing | • Active games involving running and chasing, such as flag football<br>• Bicycle riding*<br>• Jumping rope<br>• Martial arts such as karate<br>• Running<br>• Sports such as tennis, ice or field hockey, basketball, swimming, soccer<br>• Vigorous dancing<br>• Aerobics |
| **Muscle-Strengthening** | • Games such as tug of war<br>• Modified push-ups (with knees on the floor)<br>• Resistance exercises using body weight or resistance bands<br>• Rope or tree climbing<br>• Sit-ups (curl-ups or crunches)<br>• Swinging on playground equipment/bars | • Cross-country skiing<br>• Games such as tug of war<br>• Push-ups<br>• Resistance exercises with exercise bands, weight machines, hand-held weights<br>• Climbing wall<br>• Sit-ups (curl-ups or crunches) |
| **Bone-Strengthening** | • Games such as hop-scotch<br>• Hopping, skipping, jumping<br>• Jumping rope<br>• Running<br>• Sports such as gymnastics, basketball, volleyball, tennis | • Hopping, skipping, jumping<br>• Jumping rope<br>• Running<br>• Sports such as gymnastics, basketball, volleyball, tennis |

*Some activities, such as bicycling, can be moderate or vigorous intensity, depending upon level of effort.

## Ways to Promote Physical Activity in Youth

Many youth are naturally physically active and need opportunities to be active. They benefit from encouragement from parents and other adults to be active. Adults can promote youth physical activity by:

- **Providing time for both structured and unstructured physical activity during school and outside of school.**
  Children need time for active play through recess, physical activity breaks, physical education classes, after-school programs, and active time with friends and family.

- **Providing youth with positive feedback and good role models.**
  Adults should model and encourage an active lifestyle. Praise, rewards, and encouragement help youth to be active.

- **Promoting activities that set the basis for a lifetime of activity.**
  Children and adolescents should be exposed to a variety of activities: active recreation, team sports, and individual sports. In this way, they can find what they can do well in both competitive and non-competitive activities and in activities that do not require exceptional athletic skills.

# PHYSICAL EDUCATION

## PART I

*Psychomotor Development and Learning*

## Gross Motor Skills

Motor skills are deliberate and controlled movements requiring both muscle development and maturation of the central nervous system. In addition, the skeletal system must be strong enough to support the movement and weight involved in any new activity. Once these conditions are met, children learn new physical skills by practicing them until each skill is mastered.

Gross motor skills, like fine motor skills—which involve control of the fingers and hands—develop in an orderly sequence. Although norms for motor development have been charted in great detail by researchers and clinicians over the past 50 years, its pace varies considerably from one child to the next. The normal age for learning to walk has a range of several months, while the age range for turning one's head, a simpler skill that occurs much earlier, is considerably narrower. In addition to variations among children, an individual child's rate of progress varies as well, often including rapid spurts of development and frustrating periods of delay. Although rapid motor development in early childhood is often a good predictor of coordination and athletic ability later in life, there is no proven correlation between a child's rate of motor development and his intelligence. In most cases, a delay in mastering a specific motor skill is temporary and does not indicate a serious problem. However, medical help should be sought if a child is significantly behind his peers in motor development or if he regresses, losing previously acquired skills.

The sequence of gross motor development is determined by two developmental principles that also govern physical growth. The cephalo-caudal pattern, or head-to-toe development, refers to the way the upper parts of the body, beginning with the head, develop before the lower ones. Thus, infants can lift their heads and shoulders before they can sit up, which, in turn, precedes standing and walking. The other pattern of both development and maturation is proximo-distal, or trunk to extremities. One of the first things an infant achieves is head control. Although they are born with virtually no head or neck control, most infants can lift their heads to a 45-degree angle by the age of four to six weeks, and they can lift both their heads and chests at an average age of eight weeks. Most infants can turn their heads to both sides within 16 to 20 weeks and lift their heads while lying on their backs within 24 to 28 weeks. By about 36 to 42 weeks, or 9 to 10 months, most infants can sit up unassisted for substantial periods of time with both hands free for playing.

One of the major tasks in gross motor development is locomotion, or the ability to move from one place to another. An infant progresses gradually from rolling (8 to 10 weeks) to creeping on her stomach and dragging her legs behind her (6 to 9 months) to actual crawling (7 months to a year). While the infant is learning these temporary means of locomotion, she is gradually becoming able to support increasing amounts of weight while in a standing position. In the second half year of life, babies begin pulling themselves up on furniture and other stationary objects. By the ages of 28 to 54 weeks, on average, they begin "cruising," or navigating a room in an upright position by holding on to the furniture to keep their balance. Eventually, they are able to walk while holding on to an adult with both hands, and then with only one. They usually take their first uncertain steps alone between the ages of 36 and 64 weeks and are competent walks by the ages of 52 to 78 weeks. By the age of two years, children have begun to develop a variety of gross motor skills. They can run fairly well and negotiate stairs holding on to a banister with one hand and putting both feet on each step before going on to the next one. Most infants this age climb (some very actively) and have a rudimentary ability to kick and throw a ball.

During a child's first two years, most parents consider gross motor skills a very high priority; a child's first steps are the most universally celebrated developmental milestone. By the time a child is a preschooler, however, many parents shift the majority of their attention to the child's cognitive development in preparation for school. In addition, gross motor activity at these ages requires increasing amounts of space, equipment, and supervision. However, gross motor skills remain very important to a child's development, and maintaining a youngster's instinctive love of physical activity can make an important contribution to future fitness and health.

By the age of three, children walk with good posture and without watching their feet. They can also walk backwards and run with enough control for sudden stops or changes of direction. They can hop, stand on one foot, and negotiate the rungs of a jungle gym. They can walk up stairs alternating feet by usually still walk down putting both feet on each step. Other achievements include riding a tricycle and throwing a ball, although they have trouble catching it because they hold their arms out in front of their bodies no matter what direction the ball comes from. Four-year-olds can typically balance or hop on one foot, jump forward and backward over objects, and climb and descend stairs alternating feet. They can bounce and catch balls and throw accurately. Some four-year-olds can also skip. Children this age have gained an increased degree of self-consciousness about their motor activities that leads to increased feelings of pride and success when they master a new skill. However, it can also create feelings of inadequacy when they think they have failed. This concern with success can also lead them to try daring activities beyond their abilities, so they need to be monitored especially carefully.

School-age children, who are not going through the rapid, unsettling growth spurts of early childhood or adolescence, are quite skilled at controlling their bodies and are generally good at a wide variety of physical activities, although the ability varies on the level of maturation and the physique of a child. Motor skills are mostly equal in boys and girls at this stage, except that boys have more forearm strength and girls have greater flexibility. Five-year-olds can skip, jump rope, catch a bounced ball, walk on their tiptoes, balance on one foot for over eight seconds, and engage in beginning acrobatics. Many can even ride a small two-wheeler bicycle.

Eight- and nine-year-olds typically can ride a bicycle, swim, roller-skate, ice-skate, jump rope, scale fences, use a saw, hammer, and garden tools, and play a variety of sports. However, many of the sports prized by adults, often scaled down for play by children, require higher levels of distance judgment and hand-eye coordination, as well as quicker reaction times, than are reasonable for middle childhood. Games that are well-suited to the motor skills of elementary school-age children include kick ball, dodge ball, and team relay races.

In adolescence, children develop increasing coordination and motor ability. They also gain greater physical strength and prolonged endurance. Adolescents are able to develop better distance judgment and hand-eye coordination than their younger counterparts. With practice, they can master the skills necessary for adult sports.

- Eckert, Helen M. *Motor Development*. 3rd ed. Indianapolis, IN: Benchmark Press, 1987.
- Hoppert, Rita. *Rings, Swings, and Climbing Things*. Chicago: Contemporary Books, 1985.
- Lerch, Harold A., and Christine B. Stopka. *Developmental Motor Activities for All Children: From Theory to Practice*. Dubuque, IA: Brown and Benchmark, 1992.
- Thomas, Jerry R., ed. *Motor Development in Childhood and Adolescence*. Minneapolis, MN: Burgess Publishing Co., 1984.

**Maturation:** rate of progression towards an adult state which is controlled genetically by the child's biological clock.

**Growth:** change in body size that result from an increased number and size of cells.

**Experience:** external or environmental factors such as nutrition, education, and home life.

**DEVELOPMENT = maturation + growth + experience**

## Motor Development

—the increased coordination of muscles that make physical movements possible. Not just caused by maturation but also by growth and experience.

> \* early years – early motor skills (crawling, walking) are more influenced by maturation and growth.
> \* later years – later motor skills (juggling, playing volleyball) are much more influenced by genetic predisposition, exposure to knowledgeable teachers, and social factors.

Cultural differences can also affect motor skill development, although the timing and sequence of early motor skill development remains the same across all cultures.

Plyogentic skills – movements that are observed in all individuals in a group (running pattern of 8-year-old girls).

Ontogentic skills – learned skills that vary by culture and peer group (climbing a palm tree).

# Motor Learning

**Stage 1:** "getting the idea"
primarily cognitive—learner tries to "figure out" how to do the
task involves mimicking and experimentation

**Stage 2:** performance becomes stable through practice
involves drills and skill specific activities
learner can detect by not correct errors—**feedback is essential

**Stage 3:** learner performs the movement with few errors
learner can detect and correct most errors
instruction shifts from skill execution to more strategic or conceptual aspects of performance
*Autonomous Stage—learner becomes independent

The object of learning is to put correct and important information into long-term memory and for that to become knowledge. *Also, for the learner to reach Stage 3 and become independent from the teacher.

**Motor Memory:** A form of procedural memory that involves consolidating a specific motor task into memory through repetition. When a movement is repeated over time a long-term memory muscle memory is created for that task, eventually allowing it to be performed without conscious effort. This process decreases the need for attention and creates maximum efficiency within the motor and memory systems.

## Cognitive Development:
—the construction of thought processes, including remembering, problem-solving, and decision making. How a person perceives, thinks, and gains understanding of his or her world through the interaction of genetic and learned factors.

1. **Attention:** - capacity or space (short-term memory)
    - vigilance—length of time that can be allotted to attention
    - focus of attention: over-exclusive (0–5 yrs)
                              over-inclusive (5–12 yrs)
                              selective attention (12+ yrs)
2. **Information Processing:** - connect concepts
                                - abstract vs. concrete
                                - applying a name or label
3. **Rehearsal:** -practice, practice, practice
4. **Feedback**
        - extrinsic → external
        - intrinsic → internal
*Feedback sandwich: PCP—Positive, corrective, positive

## Feedback Factors
**a.** post feedback interval—time to think about the corrective information
**b.** modality—verbal, visual, and/or physical
**c.** precision—general information to specific
**d.** frequency—from a lot to less to promote the independent learner and self learner

- Feedback should cue the learner to think about and remember how movements felt.
- Feedback needs to be corrective and specific. It is not the same as reinforcement or general encouragement.

# National Standards for K-12 Physical Education

The goal of physical education is to develop physically literate individuals who have the knowledge, skills and confidence to enjoy a lifetime of healthful physical activity.

To pursue a lifetime of healthful physical activity, a physically literate individual*:

- Has learned the skills necessary to participate in a variety of physical activities.
- Knows the implications and the benefits of involvement in various types of physical activities.
- Participates regularly in physical activity.
- Is physically fit.
- Values physical activity and its contributions to a healthful lifestyle.

**Standard 1.** The physically literate individual demonstrates competency in a variety of motor skills and movement patterns.

**Standard 2.** The physically literate individual applies knowledge of concepts, principles, strategies and tactics related to movement and performance.

**Standard 3.** The physically literate individual demonstrates the knowledge and skills to achieve and maintain a health-enhancing level of physical activity and fitness.

**Standard 4.** The physically literate individual exhibits responsible personal and social behavior that respects self and others.

**Standard 5.** The physically literate individual recognizes the value of physical activity for health, enjoyment, challenge, self-expression and/or social interaction.

* Adapted from NASPE. (2004). *Moving into the future: National standards for physical education* (2nd ed.). Reston, VA: Author, and Mandigo, J., Francis, N., Lodewyk, K., & Lopez, R. (2012). Physical literacy for physical educators. *Physical Education and Health Journal*, 75 (3), 27 - 30.

Reprinted with permission from SHAPE America—Society of Health and Physical Education, 1900 Association Drive, Reston, VA 20191, www.shapeamerica.org.

*National Standards for K-12 Physical Education* (heading, rotated)

For the most recent standards please see: http://www.shapeamerica.org/standards/pe/upload/GradeLevelOutcomes_K12PE.pdf

# Elementary Physical Education Curriculum

## Movement Concepts

### Space Awareness
General or Personal Space
Direction
Level
Pathways
Planes

### Body Awareness
Shapes
Balance or Weight bearing
Transfer of Body weight
Flight

### Qualities of Movement
Time or Speed
Force
Flow

### Relationships
Among body parts
With objects and/or people
With people

Emphasis is placed on developing an understanding of movement concepts, less emphasis is place on skill technique and proper performance of skills. Students are taught correct execution of skills, but greater emphasis is placed on learning the vocabulary of movement. Creativity is to be rewarded and ingenuity reinforced.

**Space Awareness:** This category defines *where* the body can move. The spatial qualities of movement related to moving in different levels are the focus. Students are taught to use space effectively when moving.

    A. General or personal space. Personal space is the limited area individual children can use around them, and in most cases is reserved for only that student. General space is the total space that is used by all students.

    B. Direction refers to the desired route of movement, whether straight, zigzag, circular, curved, forward, backward, sideward, upward, or downward.

    C. Level defines the relationship of the body to the floor or apparatus, whether low, high, or in between.

    D. Pathways describe the path a movement takes through space. Examples include square, diamonds, triangles, circles, figure eights, etc.

    E. Planes are somewhat specific pathways defined as circular, vertical, and horizontal. All movements occur within one of the three planes.

**Body Awareness:** This category defines *what* the body can perform . . . the shapes it can make, how it can balance, and the transfer of weight to different body parts.

    A. Shapes the body makes: Many shapes can be formed with the body, such as long and short, wide or narrow, straight or twisted, stretched or curled, symmetrical or asymmetrical.

    B. Balance or weight bearing demands that different parts of the body support the weight or receive the weight. Different numbers of body parts can be involved in the movements and used as body supports.

C. Transfer of body weight is involved in the execution of many skills. Moving body weight from one part of the body to another occurs in walking, leaping, rolling, etc.

D. Flight differs from transfer of body weight in that it is explosive movement and involves lifting the body weight from the floor or apparatus for an extended period of time. The amount of time off the floor distinguishes flight from transfer of weight. Examples include running, jumping onto a climbing rope, and hanging.

**Qualities of Movement:** This category classifies *how* the body moves. The qualities of movement relate closely to mechanical principles used to move efficiently and the following, additional characteristics.

A. Time and speed deal with the speed and duration of movement. Students need to learn to move with varying speeds and to control speed throughout a variety of movements. They should also learn the relationship between body shapes and speed and be able to use body parts to generate speed. The time factor may be varied by using different speeds – moving to a constant rhythm, accelerating, and slowing down with control.

B. Force is the effort or tension generated in movement and can be used to aid in the effective execution of skills. Learning how to generate, absorb, and direct force is an important outcome. Force qualities include light, heavy, strong, weak, rough, and gentle.

C. Flow establishes how movements are purposefully sequenced to create continuity of movement. Most often this quality is discussed in terms of interrupted (bound) or sustained (free) flow. Interrupted flow stops at the end of a movement or part of a movement. Sustained flow involves smoothly linking movements or parts of a movement.

**Relationships:** This category defines with whom and/or what the body relates. A relationship is defined as the position of the performer to apparatus or other performers. Examples of relationships include; near-far, above-below, over-under, in front-behind, on-off and together-apart. When done with other students, relationships such as leading-following, mirroring-matching, and unison-opposites can be explored. Also, relationships can define the body parts as a single performer, such as arms together-apart or symmetrical-asymmetrical.

## *Fundamental Motor Skills*
### *Locomotor Skills*
### *Nonlocomotor Skills*
### *Manipulative Skills*

Fundamental skills are those utilitarian skills the children need for living and being. They also set the foundation for adult activity and form the basis for competent movement All individual, dual, and team activities use fundamental and specialized skills of one type or another. Learning fundamental skills requires an understanding of correct progressions and diligent practice. In contract to learning movement concept skills, emphasis is placed on technique rather than on creating movement variations. Fundamental motor skills should be learned under a variety of conditions and practiced in as many varied situations as possible.

**Locomotor Skills:** These skills are used to move the body from one place to another or to project the body upward. They include:

Walking
Running
Skipping
Galloping
Leaping
Jumping
Hopping
Sliding

**Nonlocomotor Skills:** These skills are performed without appreciable movement from place to place. Rather, the main purpose is movement within a small space. These include, but are not confined to:

Bending and stretching
Pushing and pulling
Twisting and turning
Rocking
Swaying
Balancing

**Manipulative Skills:** These skills involve the handling an object Most involve using the hands and feet, but other parts of the body can also be used. The manipulation of objects leads to better hand-eye and foot-eye coordination as well as dexterity. These include, but are not limited to:

Catching
Throwing
Striking
Kicking

## Specialized Motor Skills
### Body Management Skills
### Rhythmic Movement Skills
### Gymnastic Skills
### Cooperative and Personal Skills
### Game Skills
### Sport Skills

Specialized motor skills involve the use of previously learned *movement concept skills* and. *fundamental motor skills* in order to perform complex activities.

**Body Management:** These skills are required for control of the body through the integration of agility, coordination, balance, and flexibility in a variety of situations. Activities can be on large apparatus such as climbing ropes, benches, balance beams, horizontal ladders, jumping boxes, and parachutes, or small apparatus including magic ropes, tug-of-war ropes, individual mats, and gym scooters.

**Rhythmic Movement Skills:** Activities include creative rhythms, movement songs, folk dances, aerobic dance, square dance, and social dance.

**Gymnastic Skills:** (tumbling) These skills develop body management skills without the need for equipment or apparatus. Flexibility, agility, balance, strength, and body control and all enhanced through participation in gymnastics. Besides individual activities such as rolls, balances, jumps, various partner and group activities offer opportunities for social interaction and cooperation. There are six basic groups of gymnastic activities:

Animal movements
Tumbling and inverted balances
Individual stunts
Balance stunts
Partner and group stunts
Partner supports activities

**Cooperative and Personal Challenge Skills:** Cooperative skills are used to teach students to work together for the common good of other players. Activities teach cooperative skills where all students must follow specific rules and reach common goals. Relays and team challenges are part of the activities included. Personal challenges give students an opportunity to test their strength, quickness, and balance.

**Game Skills:** The purpose of game skills is to develop social skills and interactive skills such as leading, following, and making decisions. Cooperative skills that include following directions, accepting individual differences, and participating in a teamwork situation are necessary for reaching common goals. An opportunity to modify or create games is also a benefit of playing games.

**Sport Skills:** The instruction of sport skills involves teaching the specific skills, strategy and rules for a clearly defined activity. Team work and sportsmanship are stressed along with the execution of the necessary skills.

# Characteristics and Interests of Children

| TABLE 1.1 Characteristics and interests of children | |
|---|---|
| **Characteristics and Interests** | **Program Guidelines** |

**Developmental Level I**

*Psychomotor Domain*

| Characteristics and Interests | Program Guidelines |
|---|---|
| Noisy, constantly active, egocentric, exhibitionistic. Imitative and imaginative Want attention. | Include vigorous games and stunts, games with individual roles (hunting, dramatic activities, story plays), and a few team games or relays. |
| Large muscles more developed; game skills not developed. | Challenge with varied movement. Develop specialized skills of throwing, catching, and bouncing balls. |
| Naturally rhythmic. | Use music and rhythm with skills. Provide creative rhythms, folk dances, and singing movement songs. |
| May become suddenly tired but soon recover. | Use activities of brief duration. Provide short rest periods or intersperse physically demanding activities with less vigorous ones. |
| Hand-eye coordination developing. | Give opportunity to handle different objects, such as balls, beanbags, and hoops. |
| Perceptual abilities maturing. | Give practice in balance—unilateral, bilateral, and cross-lateral movements. |
| Pelvic tilt can be pronounced. | Give attention to posture problems. Provide abdominal strengthening activities. |

*Cognitive Domain*

| Characteristics and Interests | Program Guidelines |
|---|---|
| Short attention span. | Change activity often. Give short explanations. |
| Interested in what the body can do. Curious. | Provide movement experiences. Pay attention to educational movement. |
| Want to know. Often ask *why* about movement, | Explain reasons for various activities and the basis of movement. |
| Express individual views and ideas. | Allow children time to be creative. Expect problems when children are lined up and asked to perform the same task. |
| Begin to understand the idea of teamwork. | Plan situations that require group cooperation. Discuss the importance of such. |
| Sense of humor expands. | Insert some humor in the teaching process. |
| Highly creative. | Allow students to try new and different ways of performing activities; sharing ideas with friends encourages creativity. |

*Affective Domain*

| Characteristics and Interests | Program Guidelines |
|---|---|
| No gender differences in interests. | Set up same activities for boys and girls. |
| Sensitive and individualistic; self-concept very important. | Teach taking turns, sharing, and learning to win, lose, or be caught gracefully. |

*PANGRAZI, ROBERT P., DYNAMIC PHYSICAL EDUCATION FOR ELEMENTARY SCHOOL CHILDREN, 13TH, © 2001.* Printed and Electronically reproduced by permission of Pearson Education, Inc. NEW YORK, NEW YORK

| | |
|---|---|
| Accept defeat poorly. Like small-group activity. | Use entire class group sparingly. Break into smaller groups. |
| Sensitive to feelings of adults. Like to please teacher. | Give frequent praise and encouragement. |
| Can be reckless. | Stress safe approaches. |
| Enjoy rough-and-tumble activity. | Include rolling, dropping to the floor, and so on, in both introductory and program activities. Stress simple stunts and tumbling. |
| Seek personal attention. | Recognize individuals through both verbal and nonverbal means. See that all have a chance to be the center of attention. |
| Love to climb and explore play environments. | Provide play materials, games, and apparatus for strengthening large muscles (e.g., climbing towers, climbing ropes, jump ropes, miniature Challenge Courses, and turning bars). |

### Developmental Level II

#### Psychomotor Domain

| | |
|---|---|
| Capable of rhythmic movement. | Continue creative rhythms, singing movement songs, and folk dancing. |
| Improved hand-eye and perceptual-motor coordination. | Give opportunity for manipulating hand apparatus. Provide movement experience and practice in perceptual-motor skills (right and left, unilateral, bilateral, and cross-lateral movements). |
| More interest in sports. | Begin introductory sport and related skills and simple lead-up activities. |
| Sport-related skill patterns mature in some cases. | Emphasize practice in these skill areas through simple ball games, stunts, and rhythmic patterns. |
| Developing interest in fitness. | Introduce some of the specialized fitness activities to 3rd grade. |
| Reaction time slow. | Avoid highly organized ball games that require and place a premium on quickness and accuracy. |

#### Cognitive Domain

| | |
|---|---|
| Still active but attention span longer. More interest in group play. | Include active big-muscle program and more group activity. Begin team concept in activity and relays. |
| Curious to see what they can do. Love to be challenged and will try anything. | Offer challenges involving movement problems and more critical demands in stunts, tumbling, and apparatus work. Emphasize safety and good judgment. |
| Interest in group activities; ability to plan with others developing. | Offer group activities and simple dances that involve cooperation with a partner or a team. |

#### Affective Domain

| | |
|---|---|
| Like physical contact and belligerent games. | Include dodging games and other active games, as well as rolling stunts. |
| Developing more interest in skills. Want to excel. | Organize practice in a variety of throwing, catching, and moving skills, as well as others. |
| Becoming more conscious socially. | Teach need to abide by rules and play fairly. Teach social customs and courtesy in rhythmic areas. |
| Like to perform well and to be admired for accomplishments. | Begin to stress quality. Provide opportunity to achieve. |
| Essentially honest and truthful. | Accept children's word. Give opportunity for trust in game and relay situations. |
| Do not lose willingly. | Provide opportunity for children to learn to accept defeat gracefully and to win with humility. |
| Gender difference still of little importance. | Avoid separation of genders in any activity. |

# Developmental Level III

## Psychomotor Domain

| | |
|---|---|
| Steady growth. Girls often grow more rapidly than boys. | Continue vigorous program to enhance physical development. |
| Muscular coordination and skills improving. Interested in learning detailed techniques. | Continue emphasis on teaching skills through drills, lead-up games, and free practice periods. Emphasize correct form. |
| Differences in physical capacity and skill development. | Offer flexible standards so all find success. In team activities, match teams evenly so individual skill levels are less apparent. |
| Posture problems may appear. | Include posture correction and special posture instruction; emphasize effect of body carriage on self-concept. |
| Sixth-grade girls may show signs of maturity; may not wish to participate in all activities. | Have consideration for their problems. Encourage participation on a limited basis, if necessary. |
| Sixth-grade boys are rougher and stronger. | Keep genders together for skill development but separate for competition in certain rougher activities. |

## Cognitive Domain

| | |
|---|---|
| Want to know rules of games. | Include instruction on rules, regulations, and traditions. |
| Knowledgeable about and interested in sport and game strategy. | Emphasize strategy, as opposed to merely performing a skill without concern for context. |
| Question the relevance and importance of various activities. | Explain regularly the reasons for performing activities and learning various skills. |
| Desire information about the importance of physical fitness and health-related topics. | Include in lesson plans brief explanations of how various activities enhance growth and development. |

## Affective Domain

| | |
|---|---|
| Enjoy team and group activity. Competitive urge strong. | Include many team games, relays, and combatives. |
| Much interest in sports and sport-related activities. | Offer a variety of sports in season, with emphasis on lead-up games. |
| Little interest in the opposite gender. Some antagonism may arise. | Offer coeducational activities with emphasis on individual differences of all participants, regardless of gender. |
| Acceptance of self-responsibility. Strong increase in drive toward independence. | Provide leadership and followership opportunities on a regular basis. Involve students in evaluation procedures. |
| Intensive desire to excel both in skill and in physical capacity. | Stress physical fitness. Include fitness and skill surveys both to motivate and to check progress. |
| Sportsmanship a concern for both teachers and students. | Establish and enforce fair rules. With enforcement include an explanation of the need for rules and cooperation if games are to exist. |
| Peer group important. Want to be part of the gang. | Stress group cooperation in play and among teams. Rotate team positions as well as squad makeup. |

## *Instructional Design*

**PART II**

**Apple of Instructional Design**

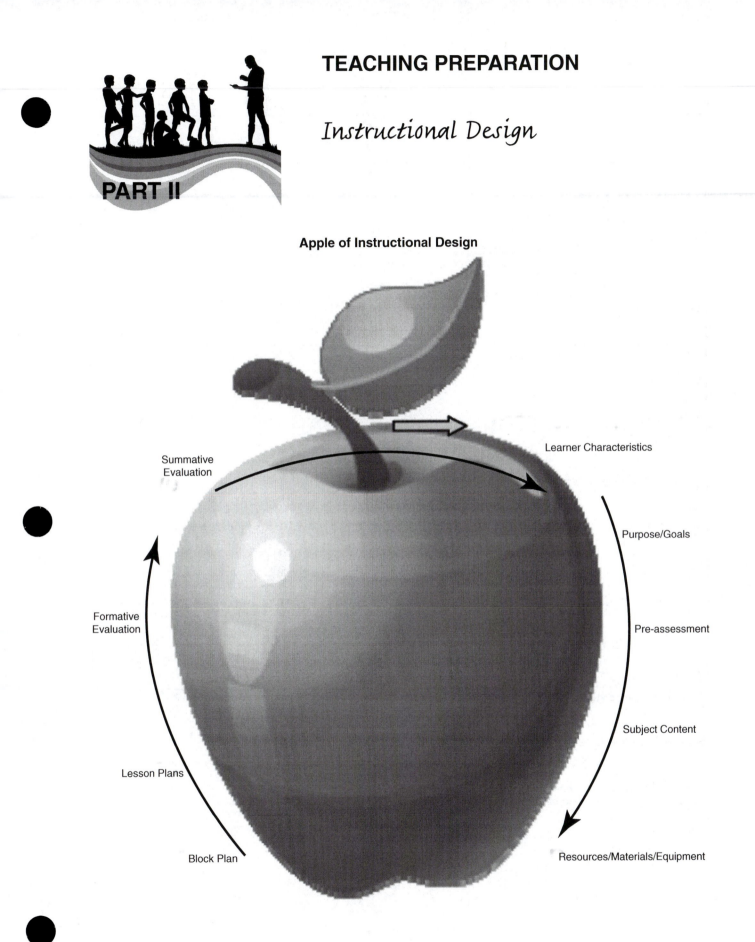

- Summative Evaluation
- Formative Evaluation
- Lesson Plans
- Block Plan
- Learner Characteristics
- Purpose/Goals
- Pre-assessment
- Subject Content
- Resources/Materials/Equipment

# Inquiry Lesson LEARNING PLAN

| Title of the lesson: | Grade/Age level: | Date: |
|---|---|---|

**Teacher Focus:**

**Scenario:**

**Iowa Core Curriculum Standards and/or Benchmarks:**

**Learning Targets** (include the stem: to introduce/practice/reteach/review/assess ... topic/skill):

**Success Criteria** ("I Can" statements):

**Procedure:** (*include a suggested **time allocation** for each part of the procedure*)

a) **Introduction** (attention getter, anticipatory set):

b) **Steps** (note technology used; List questions you will use to start conversation & possible probes):

c) **Closure** (reviewing learning, summarizing, assignments):

d) **Assessment:** (*Should be something measurable — What documentation do you have?*) **Complete these two stems:**
**Teacher will know students have met the criteria by**_____ .
                                                              (using tally sheet, comparing to rubric, anecdotal records, etc.)

**Students will**_____ .
                    Success Criteria

**Evidence of addressing diversity:** (*for example: cultural, gender, linguistic, physical, religious, sexual identity, socioeconomic, etc*)

Sample diversity statements: Calling on more boys; including music from other cultures;
While I do have diversity in SES, it is not relevant in this lesson. See the lesson on Jan. 23rd.

**Differentiation for cognitive, affective, psycho-motor needs:**

**Materials / Equipment Needed:**

**Teacher Reflection:** (*ways you will determine the success of the learning experience for learners and for you; changes you would make another time; subsequent shifts in your thinking*)

From the University of Iowa College of Education—Department of Teaching and Learning. Reprinted by permission.

| Explicit Instruction: | Grade/Age level: | Date: |
|---|---|---|

**Teacher Focus:**

**Scenario:**

**Iowa Core Curriculum Standards and/or Benchmarks:**

**Learning Targets** (include the stem: to introduce/practice/reteach/review/assess ... topic/skill):

**Success Criteria** ("I Can" statements):

**Procedure:** (*include a suggested __time allocation__ for each part of the procedure*)

a) **Introduction** (attention getter, anticipatory set):

b) **Steps** (note technology used):
**Input:**

**Model:**

**Guided Practice:**

**Independent Practice:**

c) **Closure** (reviewing learning, summarizing, assignments):

d) **Assessment:** (*Should be something measurable — What documentation do you have?*) **Complete these two stems:**
**Teacher will know students have met the criteria by**_____.
                              (using tally sheet, comparing to rubric, anecdotal records, etc.)

**Students will**_____.
          Success Criteria

**Evidence of addressing diversity:** (*for example: cultural, gender, linguistic, physical, religious, sexual identity, socioeconomic, etc*)

Sample diversity statements: Calling on more boys; including music from other cultures;
While I do have diversity in SES, it is not relevant in this lesson. See the lesson on Jan. 23rd.

**Differentiation for cognitive, affective, psycho-motor needs:** (ability level, learning style, assistive technology, etc)

**Materials / Equipment Needed:**

**Teacher Reflection:** (*ways you will determine the success of the learning experience for learners and for you; changes you would make another time; subsequent shifts in your thinking*)

# Writing Behavioral Objectives/Learning Targets

A behavioral objective has four parts:

1.  The <u>PURPOSE</u>. Why the student perform the activity? To show or demonstrate competency in what behavior?
    *   demonstrate their hand-eye coordination
    *   show their ability to absorb force
    *   demonstrate a positive attitude toward classmates
    *   show their knowledge of the rules of tennis

2.  The <u>ACTIVITY</u>. What the learner has to perform in order to demonstrate whether or not they are proficient in the purpose?
    *   juggling
    *   catching a volleyball
    *   giving positive comments
    *   answering questions

3.  The <u>CONDITIONS</u>. A specific description of the conditions under which the activity is to be performed.
    *   three scarves in a cascade pattern
    *   tossed underhand by a partner 10 feet away
    *   by the end of the class
    *   on a written multiple choice test

4.  The <u>CRITERION OF ACCEPTABILITY</u>. A specific measure to determine successful meeting of the objective. It is the measure of acceptable performance.
    *   for a minimum of 15 seconds
    *   at least 4 out of 5 times
    *   to at least five other students
    *   achieving a score of at least 80%

*   (By the end of the lesson) TLW be able to demonstrate their hand-eye coordination by juggling three scarves in a cascade pattern for a minimum of 15 seconds.
*   (By the end of the lesson) TLW be able to show their ability to absorb force by catching a volleyball, tossed underhand by a partner 10 feet away, at least 4 out of 5 times.
*   (By the end of the lesson) TLW be able to demonstrate a positive attitude toward classmates by giving positive comments to at least five other students by the end of the class.
*   (By the end of the lesson) TLW show their knowledge of the rules of tennis by achieving a score of at least 80% on a multiple choice test.

Objectives are written for all three Domains of Learning:
1.  *PHYCHOMOTOR*. Physical skills and movement.
2.  *AFFECTIVE*. Emotions, feelings.
3.  *COGNATIVE*. Mental, knowledge, thinking.

*Behavioral Objective Worksheet*

1. Identify each of the four parts in the following objectives (purpose, activity, conditions, criterion of acceptability).
   a. TLW show their cardiovascular health by running 1 mile around a track in less than 9 minutes.
   b. TLW demonstrate their understanding of the application of force by shooting a basketball jump-shot, using the correct mechanics at least 4 out of 5 times.
   c. Given a list by the teacher, TLW demonstrate their understanding of the positions on a football team by correctly identifying at least 90% of the positions on a diagram.
   d. TLW demonstrate their ability to balance by walking the length of a balance beam, without falling off, at least 4 out of 5 times.
2. Correct the following objectives by identifying the missing part(s) and rewriting it correctly.
   a. TLW demonstrate their body management skills by completing an obstacle course.
   b. TLW show their knowledge of tennis rules by achieving at least 90%.
   c. TLW demonstrate locomotor skills by using correct mechanics at least 90% of the time.
3. Write one objective for each of the three Domains of Learning.

# LOCOMOTOR MADNESS
## Lesson 3 of 5

Teacher: Carol Girdler
School: Reldrig Elementary
Date: Fall 2—

Grade: 1/2
Lesson Length: 25 minutes
Class Size: 24 students

---

**Materials:** CD#7—Locomotor Madness
CD Player

---

**Scenario/Purpose:** The class has been working on execution of locomotor skills. This lesson requires the students to integrate them with qualities of movement and rhythmic skills.

---

**Teacher Focus:** I will be working on giving corrective feedback and using "when before what."

---

**National Standards:**
Standard 1: Demonstrates competency in motor skills and movement patterns needed to perform a variety of physical activities.
Standard 3: Participates regularly in physical education.

---

**Objectives/Learning Targets:**
1. TLW demonstrate an understanding of the 8 basic locomotor movements by executing the correct skill, when names by the teacher, at least 7 out of 8 times.
2. TLW demonstrate their understanding of the mechanics of the 8 basic locomotor movements by using correct mechanics at least 90% of the time on each movement, when requested by the teacher.
3. TLW demonstrate rhythmical skills by performing a locomotor skill with qualities of movement which are appropriate to the music being played at least 90% of the time.
4. TLW show their knowledge of the qualities of movement by correctly performing the requested quality/locomotor movement, at least 90% of the time, while participating in a game of Simon Says.
5. TLW show a positive attitude toward class by willingly participating in the lesson activities 100% of the time.
6. TLW show an appreciation for classmates by giving at least 3 positive comments to other students by the end of the class period.

---

**Success Criteria:**
I can walk, run, jump, skip, hop, gallop, leap, and slide correctly.
I can move to the rhythm of music.
I can add "high-low, fast-slow, loud, and soft" to locomotor movements.

---

**Introduction:**
a) Students line up on the basketball court sideline for shoe/attire check and mental transition to class. (30 sec. max)
   *Be sure all shoes are appropriate and laces are tied.*
   *Be sure that focus is now on physical education.*
b) Warm-up.
   1. Students jog around the black lines of the basketball court in a counter clockwise direction without stopping for 2 min. 30 sec.
      *Stress jogging, not running. It is not a race.*
      *Set up CD player during the jog.*

   2. Students go to assigned squad spots after completing the jog. Squad leaders begin the routine flexibility exercises as listed below.
      • stand and reach up—both arms, then left, then right (15 sec.)
      • standing toe touches (15 sec.)

- twisties (trunk rotation) (15 sec.)
- arm circles (15 sec.)
- sitting hurdler stretches (20 sec.)
- butterflies (15 sec.)
- straddle sit & reach (15 sec.)
- 15 seconds of correct sit-ups
- 15 sec of correct curls
- * *Stress correct form—make any necessary corrections*

Total warm-up: 6 min.

Activities:
1. Students start from squad spots. Teacher will call out a locomotor movement. Students are to perform that movement moving through out the gym until told to switch to another one. (run, walk, jump, skip, hop, gallop, leap, slide)
   - call out all 8 in a random manor, using each 1 about 3 times.
   - do each movement for 5–15 seconds, varying the length of time.

   *Watch for correct movement and mechanics.*
   *Remind students to give positive comments to classmates.* (4 min)

2. Students gather and sit in front of the teacher. Review qualities of movement by having the students name examples. i.e.: high—medium—low
   - fast—medium—slow
   - loud—soft
   - big—small
   - long—short

   Explain that a variety of music will be played and that the students are to move through out the gym performing whatever locomotor movement they feel 'fits' the music and give qualities to the movement which also reflect the music. (2 min)

   *CD has a variety of music types—each segment lasts about 10–15 sec. Total tape time: 3 min.*
   *Remind students to watch out for others.*
   *Scatter students through out gym before starting.*
   *Watch for appropriateness of movements.* (3 min 30 sec)

3. Simon Says with locomotor movements/qualities of movements.
   Gather students in 1/2 of gym. Teacher will be first Simon. Call out various locomotor movements with a variety of qualities. i.e.; walk loudly, leap high, jump long, gallop soft and slow, etc.
   When a student performs without a 'simon says' they move to the other half of the gym and keep participating. Continue playing until only 3–4 students are left in the first group (have not switched to the other side). Choose 1 of the remaining students to be Simon and start another game.
   Play for approx. 8 min.

   Total activity time: 17 min 30 sec

Closure:
1. Students return to squad spots and rest quietly for 1 minute.
   *Put CD player away.*
2. Line up at door by squad lines.

Evaluation:
   Teacher will do a visual assessment of student skill based on the criterion listed in learning targets.

How have I considered diversity:
   Music played during activity 2 contains songs from a variety of countries.

**Differentiation for cognitive, affective, psychomotor needs:**

Cognitive; have students demonstrate various skills required in the lesson.

Affective; a behavior disorder student can do the activities in personal space rather than general space.

Psychomotor; a student with a physical challenge can move whatever body parts they choose.

**Teacher Reflection:**

# Boundaries

**Teacher:** Carol E. Girdler
**School:** Reldrig Elementary
**Date:** Spring, 2---

**Grade:** 5–6
**Lesson Length:** 25 minutes
**# of Students:** 20

**Scenario/Purpose:** the 5ᵗʰ/6ᵗʰ grade classes have been working on the Specialized Motor Skill of Game Skills. Although a score is kept, the important thing to take from the game is playing fair and working with teammates. The manipulative of throwing is also highlighted in this lesson.

**Teacher Focus:** I will be working on voice project and keeping my back to the wall.

**Materials:** 8—large Gator balls
4—nerf footballs
4—volleyballs
4—7" playground balls
1—6' cage ball
1—basketball
1—air pump
4—cones

## National Standards:
Standard 2; demonstrates understanding of movement concepts, principles, strategies, and tactics as they apply to the learning and performance of physical activities.
Standards 5; exhibits responsible personal and social behavior that respects self and others.

## Objectives/Learning Targets
1. TLW show their cooperative skills by contributing at least 1 idea during a team strategy session.
2. TLW demonstrate an understanding of teamwork by using the strategies agree to by the team at least 95% of the time during the game of Boundaries.
3. TLW will demonstrate their ability to adhere to rules by correctly playing by the rules described by the teacher 100% of the time.
4. TLW demonstrate good sportsmanship by acting in a positive manner toward all other classmates, whether their team wins or loses, 100% of the time.
5. TLW show their manipulative skills by using the correct mechanics for throwing a ball at least 95% of the time during the game of Boundaries.

## Success Criteria:
I can play a game using cooperation and teamwork.
I can show my sportsmanship by following the rules and being a good winner/loser.
I can throw a ball and hit a target most of the time.

## Introduction:
a) Students line up on the basketball court sideline for shoe check and mental transition to class. (30 sec. max)
    *Be sure all shoe are appropriate and laces are tied.*
    *Be sure that focus is now on physical education.*
b) Warm-up
    1. Randomly break students into groups of 5. Each group lines up single file on one side of the Basketball court, facing counter-clockwise. On go, each group follows their leader around the court, performing the locomotor skill which their leader has chosen. After 20 seconds, yell PASS. The last student in the line then speeds up enough to pass the leader. After assuming the leader position, the next student then starts performing a different locomotor skill.
    *Repeat 10 times so that each student is a leader twice. (3min. 20 sec total)*
    *Remind students that this is a warm-up and that the locomotor skills should be done at a slow pace.*
    *Set out 4 cones in a square pattern the middle of the gym approximately 10 yards apart.*
    *Get out the cage ball and pump during the warm-up and start to inflate the ball.*

2. Students go to assigned squad spots after warm-up activity #1 and perform the following stretches:
   - Stand and reach; both arms, then left arm, then right arm. (10 sec. each)
   - Arm circles, forward and backward. (10 sec. each)
   - Zipper stretch, right arm then left. (10 sec. each)
   - Shoulder pulls, left side then left. (10 sec. each)
   *Stress correct form.*
   *Continue to fill cage ball with air.*

Total warm-up: 6 min max

**Activities:**

1. Randomly put students into 4 teams of 5. After you make a group, have them go to the equipment closet and get out the following balls:
   - 2 students—each get 1 large Gator skin
   - 1 student—gets 1 football
   - 1 student—gets 1 volleyball
   - 1 student—gets 1 7" playground ball

   Next, the team should move to one side of the square and place their ball on the ground in front of them.
   *Repeat with the other 3 teams.*
   *Remind students to just carry the ball to sideline and place it on the ground in front of them.*
   *Finish inflating the cage ball and place it in the center of the square.*

Time: 2 min. 30 sec.

2. Give the following instruction/rules for the game:
   - On go, the students are to throw their balls at the cage ball, attempting to knock the ball over the boundary line of another team.
   - After they throw their ball, they can then grab any other ball around them to make another throw. The teams continue throwing at the cage ball until it rolls across another team's boundary line. As soon as the ball touches a team's boundary line, the round is over.
   - No student is allowed to touch the cage ball with part of their body.
   - No student is allowed to use a held ball to stop the forward progress of the cage ball.
   - All throws must be made from behind a team's boundary line. Throws may be overhand, underhand or side arm.
   - 1 point is awarded against the team who's boundary line is crossed by the cage ball.
   *Check for understanding of the rules.*

Time: 3 minutes

3. Play round 1.
   - have students collect all balls after the round and redistribute them so that each team will start round 2 with 2 Gator skins, 1 volleyball, 1 football, and 1 playground ball. Award point against losing team.

App Time: 2 min.

4. Allow students to strategize in teams for 1 minute before next round.
   *Place cage ball back in the middle of the square.*

5. Play round 2.
   - Repeat procedures. No strategy session after this round

App Time: 2 min.

6. Play round 3.
   - After round 3, place a basketball in the center, in place of the cage ball, and allow the teams 30 seconds for a strategy session.
   *take air out of cage ball during round 3.*

App Time: 2 min.

7. Play round 4.

App Time: 1 min.

8. Play round 5.
   • Determine winner of game (team with least points).
   • Have teams give 'high-fives' and congratulations to winning team.

App Time: 2 min<br>Total Activity Time: 16 min.

**Closure:**

1. Have all students grab 1 ball and <u>walk</u> to the storage closet. After they put the ball away in the correct place, they are to <u>walk</u> to the door to line up. (1 min.)
   *\*Put away cage ball, basketball and air pump.*
2. Use remaining time to discuss use of strategy and sportsmanship. (App 2 min.)

**Assessment:**

Teacher will do a visual assessment of the students skills based on criterion listed in objectives.

**Evidence of addressing diversity:**

Teams are picked in a random manner; not based on gender or cultural differences.

**Differentiation for cognitive, affective, psycho-motor needs:**

Cognitive; teacher can do a practice round for students who have a hard time understanding the rules.
Affective; a student who is struggling with teamwork can work with the teacher as a scorekeeper.
Psycho-motor; a student with a physical disability can still participate as a defender or strategist.

**Teacher Reflection:**

## Fitness Component

Physical fitness is now considered a measure of the body's ability to function efficiently and effectively in work and leisure activities. It includes strength, endurance, power, speed, balance, and coordination. Although every physical education class should be designed so that each student has maximum participation time, activities which are specifically targeted to enhance fitness can be added as individual challenges, small group or whole class activities. It is important to remember to keep the activities challenging but fun and enjoyable, not competitive. Students should learn that getting and staying fit is a life-long endeavor that enhances a person's overall quality of life.

## Differentiation in Instruction

The idea of differentiating instruction is an approach to teaching that advocates active planning for and attention to student differences in the context of high-quality curriculums (Tomlinson, 1999).

Differentiation allows teachers to manipulate four variables to better ensure success. The variables are:

- Content—what you teach
- Process—how you teach
- Environment—where and with what you teach
- Product—how students learning is measured

The teacher modifies the instruction to fit the needs, interests, and abilities of each student. This does not necessarily mean that instruction needs to be individualized for every student but the teacher needs to provide interrelated activities that are based on student needs for the purpose of ensuring that all students come to a similar grasp of a skill or idea (Good, 2006). This can be accomplished by choosing an activity or game with various levels of difficulty, by using task-based learning stations, by altering rules, or by providing a variety of equipment choices. The use of media, such as video clips, can also assist in differentiation.

## References

Tomlinson, C.A. (1999) *The differentiated classroom: Responding to the needs of all learners.* Alexandria, VA: Association for Supervision and Curriculum Development.

Good, M.E. (2006) *Differentiated instruction: Principles and techniques for the elementary grades.* San Rafael, CA: School of Business, Education, and Leadership at Dominican University of California. http://www.eric.ed.gov/ERICDocs/data/ericdocs2/content_storage_01/000000b/80/33/17/b4.pdf

# BLOOM'S TAXONOMY

In 1956, Benjamin Bloom headed a group of educational psychologists who developed a classification of levels of intellectual behavior important in learning.

During the 1990's a new group of cognitive psychologists, lead by Lorin Anderson (a former student of Bloom), updated the taxonomy to reflect relevance to 21st century work. The two graphics show the revised and original Taxonomy. Note the change from nouns to verbs associated with each level.

*Note that the top two levels are essentially exchanged from the traditional to the new version.*

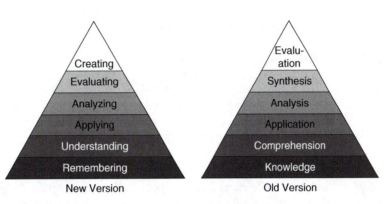

Remembering: can the student recall or remember the information?

define, duplicate, list, memorize, recall, repeat, reproduce state

Understanding: can the student explain ideas or concepts?

classify, describe, discuss, explain, identify, locate, recognize, report, select, translate, paraphrase

Applying: can the student use the information in a new way?

choose, demonstrate, dramatize, employ, illustrate, interpret, operate, schedule, sketch, solve, use, write.

Analyzing: can the student distinguish between the different parts?

appraise, compare, contrast, criticize, differentiate, discriminate, distinguish, examine, experiment, question, test.

Evaluating: can the student justify a stand or decision?

appraise, argue, defend, judge, select, support, value, evalaute

Creating: can the student create new product or point of view?

assemble, construct, create, design, develop, formulate, write.

**Some very useful sites:**

Kathy shrock's "Google Tools to Support Bloom's Revised Taxomy"

Bloom's Digital Taxonomy by Andrew Churches. This is a greally great site about how to use many different tools to enable to enhance the process of teaching students at the various levels of Bloom.

A Model of Learning Objectives. This kind of a neat site created by Rex Heer at ISU that presents a "rolloverable" 3d representation of the new 4 X 6 Taxonomy. "Rollovers" pop up simple examples of Learning Objectives. The taxonomy is also explained and links provided for even more useful resources

# Teaching Styles in Physical Education and Mosston's Spectrum

By Jonathan Doherty, *Centre for Physical Education, Leeds Metropolitan University, Leeds, UK.*

If you think back to when you were taught physical education in school, undoubtedly you will have been taught by a number of different teachers and these teachers may have had quite different instructional techniques. What is likely is that certain types of teaching appealed to you more than others, which in turn may have coloured your own thoughts about that particular sport or physical education activity. So, for example in hockey or soccer, the teacher may have used a lot of skill-drill activities where you were encouraged to practise various skills relevant to the game. In gymnastics perhaps the teacher's approach was more formal and you were expected to do exactly as that teacher instructed. The debate centres around the notion of "teaching styles" and this brief paper sets out firstly to clarify some of the confusion that exists regarding the term itself and secondly, shows how one model of teaching styles (Mosston, 1986) is an effective and creative way of teaching physical education today.

## What is meant by "teaching styles"?

The term itself has no agreed definition but the more widely accepted definitions refer to it as "a set of teaching tactics" (Galton et al, 1980) "instructional format" (Siedentop, 1991). In PE circles the definition of it as "the general pattern created by using a particular set of strategies" (BAALPE, 1989, p.9) provides a neat working definition.

Over the last thirty years a number of writers in the United Kingdom have identified particular teaching styles and related them to philosophies of teaching or to specific learning outcomes (Bennett, 1978). Emerging from this work and that of other writers specifically in PE (Kane, 1974) are two important findings. Firstly, that integral to teaching styles is its effect on the involvement of students in the learning process. Secondly, while it is acknowledged that many teachers have their own individual styles of instruction, relying on personal preference is an unstable basis for effective teaching and that selection of a teaching style must be done on a more logical and scientific basis.

By far the most detailed analysis of teaching styles and behaviours came from work originated in the United States by Mosston (1966). His ideas on the interactions between teacher and student have been developed since his initial publication and have provided a framework for teaching physical education in different contexts all over the world. So influential was it that the work that it was described as "the most significant advance in the theory of physical education pedagogy in recent history" (Nixon & Locke, 1973, p. 1227). So why is it so successful? What is it about Mosston's ideas that make them so enduring? The answer lies in the framework for teaching which he called the Spectrum of Teaching Styles.

## The Spectrum of Teaching Styles

The Spectrum established a framework of possible options in the relationship between teacher and learner (Mosston & Ashworth, 1986) and was based on the central importance of decision-making. He grouped these into *pre-impact*, impact and post-impact categories and proposed that these govern all teaching. The pre-impact set is concerned with decisions made before teaching; at preparation phase and involves subject matter, learning objectives, organisation and presentation. The *impact* set includes decisions relating to performance and execution while the post-*impact set* includes evaluation of performance and feedback from learner to teacher.

The Spectrum incorporates ten landmark styles based on the degree to which the teacher or the student assumes responsibility for what happens in a lesson. This describes a continuum, where at one extreme is the direct, teacher-led approach and at the other lies a much more open-ended and student-centred style where the teacher acts only in a facilitatory role.

## Variety is the spice of life

The Spectrum provides a sound basis for analysis of one's teaching and the effectiveness of selected styles to meet particular learning intentions. It emphasises relationships between the different styles, rather than their differences. It follows that effective instruction in PE takes account of this variety in teaching styles and an ability to use the style that is most suited to the teacher (Coates, 1997). By the same token it would be misplaced to assume that a given style is associated with a particular physical activity area or sport. The Spectrum was never intended as a straitjacket: quite

From *The New P.E. & Sports Dimension*, November 2003 by Jonathan Doherty. Copyright © 2003 by Sports Media - http://www. sports-media.org. Reprinted by permission.

the reverse. It permits a huge degree of freedom and celebrates the creativity of the individual teacher. In this way teaching is both art and science.

In teaching physical education the effective teacher is involved in adjusting and reviewing tasks set according to the needs and responses from the students. Being able to use various teaching styles identified in Mosston's framework creates an optimum working environment, maintains good discipline, sets high standards, facilitates pupils' thinking and achieves the multiple learning objectives integral to PE. Surely worthy of serious consideration in our teaching.

## References

Bennnett, N. (1978) Recent research on teaching: A dream, a belief, and a model. *British Journal of Educational Psychology*, 48, p.127–47.

British Association of Advisers and Lecturers in Physical Education (1989) *Teaching and Learning Strategies in Physical Education.* Leeds: White Line Press.

Coates, B. (1997) Refining your Style. *Sportsteacher.* Spring edition

Galton, M., Simon, B. & Croll, P. (1980) *Inside the Primary Classroom.* London: Routledge & Kegan Paul.

Kane, J.E. (1974) *Physical Education in Secondary Schools.* Schools Council Research Studies, London: Macmillan.

Mosston, M. (1966) *Teaching Physical Education.* Columbus, OH: Merrill.

Mosston, M. & Ashworth, S. (1986) *Teaching Physical Education.* Columbus, OH: Merrill.

Nixon, J. & Locke, L. (1973) Research on teaching physical education. In R. Travers (Ed.), *Handbook of research on teaching*, pp. 1210–1242. Chicago: Rand McNally.

Siedentop, D. (1991) *Developing Teaching Skills in Physical Education.* Palo Alto, CA: Mayfield.

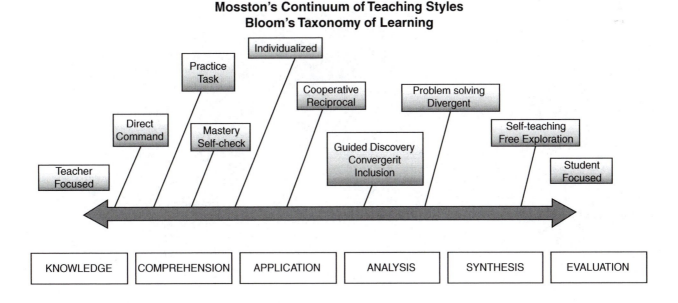

# Classroom Management

1. **Control Word**—*Freeze*
2. **'When before What'**
3. **'Back To The Wall'**
4. **Student Management**
   - why do students misbehave?
   (least disruptive to more disruptive)
   a. **the look**
   b. **proximity**
   c. **pause with look**
   d. **use of name within information**
   e. **check for understanding—open ended question (vs. closed)**
   f. **direct comments**
   g. **new placement or separation**
   h. **time out**
   i. **principal's office**
5. **Keep equipment out of student's hands when giving directions.**
6. **Be sure that all students are stopped, facing you, and listening when you give instructions.**

## Conflict Resolution

Too many of our young people are caught up in conflicts every day that they do not know how to manage–teasing, jealousy, and physical aggression. Juvenile delinquency and violence are symptoms of youth's inability to manage conflict in their lives. Teaching youth how to manage conflict in a productive way can help reduce incidents of violent behavior. Conflict resolution education is a beneficial component of a comprehensive violence prevention and intervention program in schools and communities.

Conflict resolution education encompasses problem solving in which the parties in dispute express their points of view, voice their interests, and find mutually acceptable solutions. Conflict resolution education programs help the parties recognize that while conflict happens all the time, people can learn new skills to deal with conflict in nonviolent ways. The programs that appear to be most effective are comprehensive and involve multiple components such as the problem–solving processes and principles of conflict resolution, the basics of effective communication and listening critical and creative thinking, and an emphasis on personal responsibility and self-discipline.

According to William Delong, a lecturer at the Harvard School of Public Health. "The best school-based violence prevention programs seek to do more than reach the individual child. They instead try to change the total school environment, to create a safe community that lives by a credo of non-violence and multicultural appreciation."[1] Most school violence-prevention programs include conflict resolution education.

Effective conflict resolution education programs can:
- Enable children to respond nonviolently to conflict by using the conflict resolution problem-solving processes of negotiation, mediation, and consensus decisionmaking.
- Enable educators' ability to manage students' behavior without coercion by emphasizing personal responsibility and self-discipline.
- Mobilize community involvement in violence prevention through education programs and services, such as expanding the role of youth as effective citizens beyond the school into the community.

## Four Common Strategies for Approaching Conflict Resolution

Experts identify four school-based conflict resolution strategies that can be replicated in other settings. These are commonly referred to as: (1) Peer Mediation, (2) Process Curriculum, (3) Peaceable Classrooms, and (4) Peaceable Schools. The Peaceable Schools model incorporates the elements of the other three approaches. In all four approaches, conflict resolution education is viewed as giving youth nonviolent tools to deal with daily conflicts that can lead to self-destructive and violent behaviors. It is up to each local school district to decide how conflict resolution education will be integrated into its overall educational environment. The expectation is that when youth learn to recognize and constructively address what takes place before conflict or differences lead to violence, the incidence and intensity of that situation will diminish.

The program examples provided below empower young people with the processes and skills of conflict resolution. However, youth need to know then conflict resolution does not take precedence over adult responsibility to provide the final word in a variety of circumstances or situations. Conflict resolution has a place in the home, school, and community, but it can only supplement, not supplant, adult authority.

**Peer Mediation Approach:** Recognizing the importance of directly involving youth in conflict resolution, many schools and communities are using the Peer Mediation approach. Under this approach specially trained student mediators work with their peers to resolve conflicts Mediation programs reduce the use of traditional disciplinary actions such as suspension, determine, and expulsion, encourage effective problem solving: decrease the need for teacher involvement in student conflicts: and improve school climate. An example of a Peer Mediation program is We Can Work It Out, developed by the National Institute for Citizenship Education in the Law and the National Crime Prevention Council. The program promotes mediation, negotiation, or other non-litigating methods as strategies to settle unresolved confrontations and fighting.

One Albuquerque elementary school principal reported. "We were having 100 to 150 fights every month on the playground before we started the New Mexico Center for Dispute Resolution's Mediation in the Schools Program. By the end of the school year, we were having maybe 10 (fights)."[2] Other elementary schools using the same Peer Mediation approach to conflict resolution education reported that playground fighting had been reduced to such an extent that peer mediators found themselves out of a job.

**Process Curriculum Approach:** Teachers who devote a specific time—a separate course, a distinct curriculum or a daily lesson—to the principles, foundation abilities, and problem-solving processes of conflict resolution are implementing the Process Curriculum approach. The Program for Young Negotiators, based on the Harvard Negotiation Project, is representative of this approach. Participating students, teacher, and administrators are taught how to use principled negotiation to achieve goals and resolve disputes. This type of negotiation helps disputants envision scenarios and generate options for achieving results that satisfy both sides.

In a North Caroline middle school with more than 700 students, conflict resolution education was initiated. The school used the Peace Foundation's Fighting Fair curriculum and a combination of components from various conflict resolution projects. After a school year, in-school suspensions decreased from 52 to 30 incidents (a 42-percent decrease), and out-of-school suspensions decreased from 40 incidents to 1 (a 97-percent decrease).[3]

**Peaceable Classroom Approach:** The Peaceable Classroom approach integrates conflict resolution into the curriculum and daily management of the classroom. It uses the instructional methods of cooperative learning and "academic controversy." The Educators for Social Responsibility curriculum. Making Choices About Conflict, Security, and Peacemaking, is a peaceable classroom management, and discipline practices. It emphasizes opportunities to practice cooperation, appreciation of diversity, and caring and effective communication. Generally, peaceable classrooms are initiated on a teacher-by-teacher basis into the classroom setting and are the building blocks of the peaceable school.

Studies on the effectiveness of the Teaching Students To Be Peacemakers program a Peaceable Classroom approach to conflict resolution, show that discipline problems requiring teacher management decreased by approximately 80 percent and referrals to the principal were reduced to zero.[4]

**Peaceable School Approach:** The Peaceable School approach incorporates the above three approaches. This approach seeks to create schools when conflict resolution has been adopted by every member of the school community, from the crossing guard to the classroom teacher. A peaceable school promotes a climate that challenges youth and adults to believe and act on the understanding that a diverse, nonviolent society is a realistic goal. In Creating the Peaceable School Program of the Illinois Institute for Dispute Resolution, students are empowered with conflict resolution skills and strategies to regulate and control their own behavior. Conflict resolution is infused into the way business is conducted at the school between students, between students and teachers and other personnel, between teachers and administrators, and between parents and teachers and administrators.

In an evaluation of the Resolving Conflict Creatively Program in four multiethnic school districts in New York City, teachers of the Peaceable School approach to conflict resolution reported a 71-percent decrease in physical violence in the classroom and observed 66 percent less name calling and fewer verbal insults.[5] Other changes in student behavior reported by the teachers included greater acceptance of differences, increased awareness and articulation of feelings, and a spontaneous use of conflict resolution skills throughout the school day in a variety of academic and nonacademic settings.

## Conflict Resolution Education in Other Settings

The usefulness of conflict resolution programs is not limited to traditional school settings. These programs are also a meaningful component of safe and violence-free juvenile justice facilities and alternative education programs. In these settings, conflict resolution programs are introduced not to replace but to supplement existing disciplinary policies and procedures. When opportunities are created to learn and practice conflict resolution principles and strategies in these settings, youth may receive positive life skills and acquire behaviors to carry with them throughout their lives. No longer do they need to feel that a crosswise look or a cutting remark requires a physical challenge that can lead to violent outcomes. They learn to control their anger and to react in a nonconfrontational manner to diffuse the situation. When youth practice conflict resolution principles and skills on a regular basis, they begin to experience greater satisfaction in their lives.

The Youth Corrections Mediation Program of the New Mexico Center for Dispute Resolution teaches youth and staff in juvenile justice facilities communication skills and combines the conflict resolution curricula with mediation. This program has a reintegration component in which families negotiate agreements for daily living before the juvenile offenders return home. The program emphasizes the need to model and practice communication and the problem-solving processes of conflict resolution. By providing alternatives to resolving conflicts, the program gives youth a model for positive expression and the peaceful resolution of problems. An evaluation study of the program reported a 37-percent decrease in disciplinary infractions among youth mediators compared with 12-percent for youth not trained as mediators. This study also found that the recidivism rate among youth trained as mediators was 18-percent lower during the first 6 months after returning to the community than for a control group not trained in mediation.[6] The knowledge and skills of conflict resolution give these former offenders the tools to defuse or resist conflict situations and get along better with family, friends, teachers, supervisors, and fellow students or fellow employees.

Taking what they have gleaned back into the community and family settings is often the biggest challenge young people face with conflict resolution training, especially when others are not similarly trained. A number of conflict resolution education programs have either originated in the community and moved into the school or moved from the school into the community. Regardless of their origin, the programs enhance the quality of life in the home, school, and community. Parent and community conflict resolution education programs build on and complement the school program. These programs provide common vocabulary and problem-solving processes that serve as critical linkages for youth who have been trained in conflict resolution in schools.

## Community Mediation Centers

Community mediation centers are located in more than 400 communities across the country. These centers which are typically nonprofit community-based agencies, use trained community volunteers to provide a wide range of mediation services to youth and adults. Through these centers, mediation has been applied in common conflict situations found in the community, schools, and families, such as gangs, business complaints of juvenile loitering, school suspensions, truancy, and parent/child relationships, as well as in juvenile justice settings. Community mediation centers also offer training in conflict resolution processes and skills that may be used effectively in personal and professional life for all age groups. Nationwide community mediation centers have collaborated with law enforcement, schools, and other youth-serving agencies in developing and implementing community-based comprehensive violence prevention and intervention programs. A listing of local community mediation centers is available from the National Association for Community Mediation. (See contact information under "Resources.")

## Conclusion

The effective conflict resolution education programs highlighted above have helped to improve the climate in school, community and juvenile justice settings by reducing the number of disruptive and violent acts in these settings by decreasing the number of chronic school absences due to a fear of violence by reducing the number of disciplinary referrals and suspensions: by increasing academic instruction during the school days and by increasing the self-esteem and self-respect, as well as the personal responsibility and self-discipline of the young people involved in these programs.

Young people cannot be expected to promote and encourage the peaceful resolution of conflicts if they do not see conflict resolution principles and strategies being modeled by adults in all areas of their lives such as in business, sports, entertainment, and personal relationships. Adults play a part in making the environment more peaceful by practicing nonviolent conflict resolution when minor or major disputes arise in their daily lives.

## Resources

Providing guidance on conflict resolution education programs, the Office of Juvenile Justice and Delinquency Prevention (OJJDP) of the Department of Justice, in partnership with the Safe and Drug-Free Schools Program of the Department of Education, has developed a guide entitled *Conflict Resolution Education: A Guide to Implementing Programs in Schools. Youth-Serving Organizations, and Community and Juvenile Justice Settings.* The guide is designed to be a tool for teachers, administrators, school board members school site-based management teams, and youth-serving and juvenile justice professionals to use in their strategic planning for implementing conflict resolution education programs that meet their specific needs. It also includes a reading list and annotated lists of conflict resolution programs by approach, resources, and trainers with contact information. In addition to the guide, OJJDP has a videotape from a satellite teleconference on conflict resolution education, which was based on the guide. Experts and practitioners in conflict resolution discussed the benefits and importance of teaching youth the skills to resolve disputes without violence. Model programs across the country were showcased. To receive a copy of either the guide or videotape, contact OJJDP's Juvenile Justice Clearinghouse at 800-638-8736.

For information on local community mediation centers, contact the National Association for Community Mediation at 1726 M Street, NW Suite 500, Washington, DC 20036 or at 202-167-1769, and by fax at 202-166-1769.

For information on establishing conflict resolution programs for schools and a list of best practices, contact. Safe and Drug-Free Schools Program, U.S. Department of Education, Washington, DC 20202, 202-260-3934.

# Multicultural/Gender Fair Curriculum

## Referencing Education Standard

12.5(8) Multicultural and gender fair approaches to the educational program. The board shall establish a policy to ensure that students are free from discriminatory practices in the educational program as required by Iowa Code section 256.11. In developing or revising the policy, parents, students, instructional and non-instructional staff, and community members shall be involved. Each school or school district shall incorporate multicultural and gender fair goals for the educational program into its comprehensive school improvement plan. Incorporation shall Include the following:

a. Multicultural approaches to the educational program. These shall be defined as approaches which foster knowledge of, and respect and appreciation for, the historical and contemporary contributions of diverse cultural groups, including race, color, national origin, gender, disability, religion, creed, and socioeconomic background. The contributions and perspectives of Asian Americans, African Americans, Hispanic Americans, American Indians, European Americans, and persons with disabilities shall be included in the program.
b. Gender fair approaches to the educational program. These shall be defined as approaches, which foster knowledge of, and respect and appreciation for, the historical and contemporary contributions of women and men to society. The program shall reflect the wide variety of roles open to both women and men and shall provide equal opportunity to both sexes.

Approved by the Iowa Department of Education and Iowa Legislation

## Cross-Curricular/Interdisciplinary Content

Cross-curricular/interdisciplinary content requires a conscious effort by a teacher to apply the knowledge, concepts, and/or principles of more than one academic curriculum area at the same time. It is often seen as a way to address fragmentation and isolated skill instruction and as a way to assist in such things as transfer of learning, teaching students to think and reason, and providing a curriculum that is more relevant to students.

# Inclusion in Physical Education

Classes which help all students participate fully regardless of physical, cognitive, or emotional challenges. Includes students who may face barriers due to:

- Language
- Body composition
- Gender
- Cultural or religious background

### Inclusive classroom (gym)
- Where all students feel a sense of belonging
- Where students feel supported by peers
- Where instruction is in a Least Restrictive Environment (LRE)

The 4 S's of Inclusive Physical Education (Reeves & Stein, 1999)
1. Safe—from physical, psychological, or emotional dangers, including bullying or embarrassment
2. Satisfying—adapt activities so that all students feel personally challenged and motivated
3. Successful—all students can obtain an appropriate level of proficiency
4. Skill-appropriate—consideration of developmental status, fitness level, skill level, body size, and age of each student

## Students with disabilities
Federal Law PL 94-192, PL 101-476, PL 105-17
- Mandates that physical education be provided to students with disabilities.
- Includes development of:
  1. Physical and motor skills
  2. Fundamental motor skills
  3. Specialized motor skills—aquatics, dance, games, sports skills, etc.

# Inclusion in physical Education

### Individualize the Task Demands of an Activity:
1. The Movement Form
   - modify or substitute the movement involved—find a slightly different movement that may be more appropriate.

   ***Instead of running or walking;***
   - walking with a partner
   - crawling/walking on all fours
   - riding a tricycle
   - using a wheelchair

   ***Instead of throwing or kicking a ball;***
   - rolling a ball along the floor
   - dropping or releasing a ball at a certain marker
   - carrying a ball to a spot

   ***Instead of catching a ball;***
   - blocking a ball using their body
   - using equipment to trap or capture the ball

2. Adapting the Environment
   - organizing the playing area so various forms of mobility can be used
   • ensure there is a good floor surface
   • use chairs
   • use gym mats
3. Adapting the Equipment
   • size/weight/texture of ball
   • use strapping to hold racquets
   • make targets or goals larger/higher/lower
   • use equipment to strike instead of throw or kick
4. Adapting Rules or Instructions
   • have fewer
   • use pictures or symbols
   • use a buddy system

# Process-Product Evaluation

**Second Grade—Standard 1: Students demonstrate the motor skills and movement patterns needed to perform a variety of physical activities.**

Name:_____ Observer: _____ Date: _____

| Locomotor Movement 1.5 1.6 | Using Proper From (UPF) | Incorrect Form | Notes |
|---|---|---|---|
|  | 1 2 3 4 5<br>6 7 8 9 10 | 1 2 3 4 5<br>6 7 8 9 10 |  |
|  | 1 2 3 4 5<br>6 7 8 9 10 | 1 2 3 4 5<br>6 7 8 9 10 |  |
|  | 1 2 3 4 5<br>6 7 8 9 10 | 1 2 3 4 5<br>6 7 8 9 10 |  |
|  | 1 2 3 4 5<br>6 7 8 9 10 | 1 2 3 4 5<br>6 7 8 9 10 |  |
|  | 1 2 3 4 5<br>6 7 8 9 10 | 1 2 3 4 5<br>6 7 8 9 10 |  |
|  | 1 2 3 4 5<br>6 7 8 9 10 | 1 2 3 4 5<br>6 7 8 9 10 |  |
|  | 1 2 3 4 5<br>6 7 8 9 10 | 1 2 3 4 5<br>6 7 8 9 10 |  |
|  | 1 2 3 4 5<br>6 7 8 9 10 | 1 2 3 4 5<br>6 7 8 9 10 |  |
|  | 1 2 3 4 5<br>6 7 8 9 10 | 1 2 3 4 5<br>6 7 8 9 10 |  |

_____

From Physical Education: Standards Based Assessment Thomas C. Minniear © 2007 Kendall Hunt Publishing Company. Reprinted by permission.

**Fourth Grade: Standard 2: Students demonstrate knowledge of movement concepts, principles, and strategies that apply to the learning and performance of physical activities.**

Name: _____ Observer: _____ Date: _____

| | Satisfactory | Unsatisfactory | A | B | C | D | F |
|---|---|---|---|---|---|---|---|
| 2.1 Explain the difference between offense and defense. | | | | | | | |
| 2.2 Describe ways to create more space between an offensive player and a defensive player. | | | | | | | |
| 2.3 Describe the appropriate body orientation to serve a ball, using the underhand movement pattern. | | | | | | | |
| 2.4 Describe the appropriate body orientation to strike a ball, using the forehand movement pattern. | | | | | | | |
| 2.5 Explain the similar movement elements of the underhand throw and the underhand volleyball serve. | | | | | | | |
| 2.6 Distinguish between punting and kicking and describe the similarities and differences. | | | | | | | |
| 2.7 Compare and contrast dribbling a ball without a defender and with a defender. | | | | | | | |
| 2.8 Explain the differences in manipulating an object when using a long-handled implement and when using a short-handled implement. | | | | | | | |

*(Continued)*

| | Satisfactory | Unsatisfactory | A | B | C | D | F |
|---|---|---|---|---|---|---|---|
| 2.9 Identify key body positions used for volleying a ball. | | | | | | | |
| 2.10 Design a routine to music that includes even and uneven locomotor patterns. | | | | | | | |

**Comments:**

_____

_____

_____

_____

## Scoring Rubric—Overhand Throwing (Process Evaluation)

| | Always (4) | Most of the Time (3) | Some of the Time (2) | Seldom (1) | Never (0) | Comments |
|---|---|---|---|---|---|---|
| Ball is held in fingertips | | | | | | |
| Rotation of body towards dominant side | | | | | | |
| Ball side elbow moves back, past ear | | | | | | |
| Step toward target on nondominant foot | | | | | | |
| Rotation of body toward center line as dominant arm moves forward | | | | | | |
| Extension of arm, followed by snap of wrist | | | | | | |
| Follow through toward target | | | | | | |

# Physical Education Teaching Hints

1. Be organized. Have equipment ready and move students through transitions quickly.

2. Explain what the activity is, and how to do it. Give simple cues that convey both the concept being taught and the specifics for execution. Remember, most students learn best by doing, not listening. Keep directions clear and concise, and use visual as well as verbal directions. Use KIS philosophy.

3. Always keep safety in mind. Consider the facility, the equipment, the activity, and the organizational pattern of the students. Keep your "back to the wall."

4. Provide short, frequent practice sessions for beginning students. Bored or tired students will perform poorly.

5. Give constant feedback. Circulate throughout the facility, try and reach every student at least once during the class period. Be as specific as possible with comments.

6. Keep the maximum number of students active for the maximum amount of time.

7. Be enthusiastic! If you want the students to be excited about learning and to give a good effort, then you need to convey this in your voice and mannerisms.

8. Be sure the activity relates to the lesson focus and the level of difficulty doesn't hinder execution of the focus.

9. Be flexible—don't teach to time. If students have satisfied the objective, move on. If students are struggling or seem confused, reteach or modify the activity.

10. Use a key word or sound to gain immediate attention from the class.

11. Use a normal voice as much as possible. Stop student activity when you need to give instructions or corrections. If you yell too much, active students will either not hear you or will tune you out. Besides, your voice will give out and you'll end up with a headache.

12. Remember— each individual is different, and there is no one best method that applies to all students, teachers, or activities.

13. Give directions to one activity, have the students perform that activity, then give directions to the next activity.

14. Have younger students repeat numbers; have older students say numbers.

# 10 SIMPLE ACTIVITIES TO ENCOURAGE PHYSICAL ACTIVITY IN THE CLASSROOM

1. Secret Password: Every day establish a secret password activity such as 5 jumping jacks, stand on one foot for 5 seconds, hop three times, etc. Then establish when the student needs to use the secret password - i.e. after a drink of water, before receiving a hand out, when entering the classroom, in between subjects, etc.

2. Walking Worksheets: Tape worksheets on wall, easel and chalkboard.  Students move from worksheet to worksheet and answer the different questions.

3. Opposite Hunt: Divide the class in half.  Half of the class write a word on an index card.  The other half writes the definition.  Shuffle the cards and hand one card to each student.  The students must move around the classroom and match the word with the definition.  For younger students match up sight words, letter or numbers.  Try math problems and solutions.

4. Pencil Jumps: For a quick movement break in between lessons have each student place a pencil on the floor.  Jump over the pencil a designated number of times.

5. Race in Place: When reviewing material, have the students stand up and run in place by their desks.  On the teacher's signal, student stops running in place, listens to question and writes down the answer on paper.

6. Daily Rule: Establish a new daily rule every day that includes physical activity.  I.e. walk backwards to water fountain, tip toe to the bathroom, stretch before sitting in chair.  See if you can catch the students forgetting the daily rule.

7. Shredder: Cut up worksheets in quarters.  Students can help scatter the worksheets around the floor face down.  On the teacher's signal, the students can crawl around the floor, find the four quarters of the worksheet, complete the worksheet and give it to teacher.

8. Push Up Line Up: When the students line up against the wall to leave the classroom, have each student face the wall and perform 10 wall push ups.  After all push ups completed the class can walk in the line.

9. Mobile Math: Divide the class in half to review math problems. The students can stand at their desks (paper and pencil on desk).  Call out a math problem such as 4+5=.  One half of the class jumps 4 times and the other half jumps five times.  Each student writes down answer on paper. Continue with other math problems.  Vary movements.

10. Q and A Stretching:  Provide students with paper at desk. Students can stand or sit.  Ask a question and student writes down the answer (very large) on one sheet of paper.  Each student holds paper up, with two hands overhead to stretch. Teacher checks answers.  Multiple choice questions work best.

**Looking for more motor activity ideas??  Visit**
# www.YourTherapySource.com

© 2007 Your Therapy Source, Inc.

**HEALTH**

# National Health Education Standards

## PART III

**HEALTH EDUCATION STANDARD 1—Students will comprehend concepts related to health promotion and disease prevention to enhance health.**

## Rationale

The acquisition of basic health concepts and functional health knowledge provides a foundation for promoting health-enhancing behaviors among youth. This standard includes essential concepts that are based on established health behavior theories and models. Concepts that focus on both health promotion and risk reduction are included in the performance indicators.

## Performance Indicators

| Pre-K-2 | 3–5 | 6–8 | 9–12 |
|---|---|---|---|
| 1.2.1. identify that healthy behaviors impact personal health | 1.5.1 describe the relationship between healthy behaviors and personal health. | 1.8.1. analyze the relationship between healthy behaviors and personal health. | 1.12.1 predict how healthy behaviors can impact health status. |
| 1.2.2. recognize that there are multiple dimensions of health. | 1.5.2 identify examples of emotional, intellectual, physical, and social health. | 1.8.2. describe the inter-relationship of emotional, intellectual, physical, and social health in adolescence. | 1.12.2. describe the interrelationships of emotional, intellectual, physical, and social health. |
| 1.2.3. describe ways to prevent communicable diseases. | 1.5.3. describe ways in which a safe and healthy school and community environment can promote personal health. | 1.8.3. analyze how the environment impacts personal health. | 1.12.3. analyze how environment and personal health are interrelated. |
| | | 1.8.4. describe how family history can impact personal health. | 1.12.4. analyze how genetics and family history can impact personal health. |
| 1.2.4. list ways to prevent common childhood injuries. | 1.5.4. describe ways to prevent common childhood injuries and health problems. | 1.8.5. describe ways to reduce or prevent injuries and other adolescent health problems. | 1.12.5. propose ways to reduce or prevent injuries and health problems. |
| 1.2.5. describe why it is important to seek health care. | 1.5.4. describe when it is important to seek health care. | 1.8.6. explain how appropriate health care can promote personal health. | 1.12.6. analyze the relationship between access to health care and health status. |

*continued*

| Pre-K-2 | 3–5 | 6–8 | 9–12 |
|---------|-----|-----|------|
| | | 1.8.7. describe the benefits of and barriers to practicing healthy behaviors. | 1.12.7. compare and contrast the benefits of and barriers to practicing a variety of healthy behaviors. |
| | | 1.8.8. examine the likelihood of injury or illness if engaging in unhealthy behaviors. | 1.12.8. analyze personal susceptibility to injury, illness or death if engaging in unhealthy behaviors. |
| | | 1.8.9. examine the potential seriousness of injury or illness if engaging in unhealthy behaviors. | 1.12.9. analyze the potential severity of injury or illness if engaging in unhealthy behaviors. |

**HEALTH EDUCATION STANDARD 2—Students will analyze the influence of family, peers, culture, media, technology and other factors on health behaviors.**

## Rationale

Health is impacted by a variety of positive and negative influences within society. This standard focuses on identifying and understanding the diverse internal and external factors that influence health practices and behaviors among youth including personal values, beliefs and perceived norms.

## Performance Indicators

| Pre-K-2 | 3–5 | 6–8 | 9–12 |
|---------|-----|-----|------|
| 2.2.1 identify how the family influences personal health practices and behaviors. | 2.5.1 describe how family influences personal health practices and behaviors. | 2.8.1 examine how the family influences the health of adolescents. | 2.12.1 analyze how family influences the health of individuals. |
| | 2.5.2. identify the influence of culture on health practices and behaviors | 2.8.2. describe the influence of culture on health beliefs, practices and behaviors. | 2.12.2. analyze how culture supports and challenges health beliefs, practices and behaviors. |
| | 2.5.3. identify how peers can influence healthy and unhealthy behaviors. | 2.8.3. describe how peers influence healthy and unhealthy behaviors. | 2.12.3. analyze how peers influence healthy and unhealthy behaviors. |
| 2.2.2. identify what the school can do to support personal health practices and behaviors. | 2.5.4. describe how the school and community can support personal health practices and behaviors. | 2.8.4. analyze how the school and community can impact personal health practices and behaviors. | 2.12.4. evaluate how the school and community can impact personal health practice and behaviors. |
| 2.2.3. describe how the media can influence health behaviors. | 2.5.5. explain how media influences thoughts, feelings, and health behaviors. | 2.8.5. analyze how messages from media influence health behaviors. | 2.12.5. evaluate the effect of media on personal and family health. |
| | 2.5.6. describe ways technology can influence personal health. | 2.8.6. analyze the influence of technology on personal and family health. | 2.12.6. evaluate the impact of technology on personal, family and community health. |
| | | 2.8.7. explain how the perceptions of norms influence healthy and unhealthy behaviors. | 2.12.7. analyze how the perceptions of norms influence healthy and unhealthy behaviors. |
| | | 2.8.8. explain the influence of personal values and beliefs on individual health practices and behaviors. | 2.12.8. analyze the influence of personal values and beliefs on individual health practices and behaviors. |

*continued*

| Pre-K-2 | 3–5 | 6–8 | 9–12 |
|---------|-----|-----|------|
|         |     | 2.8.9. describe how some health risk behaviors can influence the likelihood of engaging in unhealthy behaviors. | 2.12.9. analyze how some health risk behaviors can influence the likelihood of engaging in unhealthy behaviors. |
|         |     | 2.8.10. explain how school and public health policies can influence health promotion and disease prevention. | 2.12.10. analyze how public health policies and government regulations can influence health promotion and disease prevention. |

**HEALTH EDUCATION STANDARD 3—Students will demonstrate the ability to access valid information and products and services to enhance health.**

## Rationale

Accessing valid health information and health-promoting products and services is critical in the prevention, early detection, and treatment of health problems. This standard focuses on how to identify and access valid health resources and to reject unproven sources. Applying the skills of analysis, comparison and evaluation of health resources empowers students to achieve health literacy.

## Performance Indicators

| Pre-K-2 | 3–5 | 6–8 | 9–12 |
|---|---|---|---|
| 3.2.1. identify trusted adults and professionals who can help promote health. | 3.5.1. identify characteristics of valid health information, products and services. | 3.8.1. analyze the validity of health information, products and services. | 3.12.1. evaluate the validity of health information, products and services. |
| 3.2.2. identify ways to locate school and community health helpers. | 3.5.2. locate resources from home, school and community that provide valid health information. | 3.8.2. access valid health information from home, school, and community. | 3.12.2. utilize resources from home, school and community that provide valid health information. |
| | | 3.8.3. determine the accessibility of products that enhance health. | 3.12.3. determine the accessibility of products and services that enhance health. |
| | | 3.8.4. describe situations that may require professional health services. | 3.12.4. determine when professional health services may be required. |
| | | 3.8.5. locate valid and reliable health products and services. | 3.12.5. access valid and reliable health products and services. |

**HEALTH EDUCATION STANDARD 4—Students will demonstrate the ability to use interpersonal communication skills to enhance health and avoid or reduce health risks.**

## Rationale

Effective communication enhances personal, family, and community health. This standard focuses on how responsible individuals use verbal and non-verbal skills to develop and maintain healthy personal relationships. The ability to organize and to convey information and feelings is the basis for strengthening interpersonal interactions and reducing or avoiding conflict.

## Performance Indicators

| Pre-K-2 | 3–5 | 6–8 | 9–12 |
|---------|-----|-----|------|
| 4.2.1. demonstrate healthy ways to express needs, wants and feelings. | 4.5.1. demonstrate effective verbal and non-verbal communication skills to enhance health. | 4.8.1. apply effective verbal and nonverbal communication skills to enhance health. | 4.12.1. utilize skills for communicating effectively with family, peers, and others to enhance health. |
| 4.2.2. demonstrate listening skills to enhance health. | 4.5.2. demonstrate refusal skills to avoid or reduce health risks. | 4.8.2. demonstrate refusal and negotiation skills to avoid or reduce health risks. | 4.12.2. demonstrate refusal, negotiation, and collaboration skills to enhance health and avoid or reduce health risks. |
| 4.2.3. demonstrate ways to respond when in an unwanted, threatening or dangerous situation. | 4.5.3. demonstrate non-violent strategies to manage or resolve conflict. | 4.8.3. demonstrate effective conflict management or resolution strategies. | 4.12.3. demonstrate strategies to prevent, manage or resolve interpersonal conflicts without harming self or others |
| 4.2.4. demonstrate ways to tell a trusted adult if threatened or harmed. | 4.5.4. demonstrate how to ask for assistance to enhance personal health. | 4.8.4. demonstrate how to ask for assistance to enhance the health of self and others. | 4.12.4. demonstrate how to ask for and offer assistance to enhance the health of self and others. |

**HEALTH EDUCATION STANDARD 5—Students will demonstrate the ability to use decision-making skills to enhance health.**

## Rationale

Decision-making skills are needed in order to identify, implement and sustain health-enhancing behaviors. This standard includes the essential steps needed to make healthy decisions as prescribed in the performance indicators. When applied to health issues, the decision-making process enables individuals to collaborate with others to improve quality of life.

## Performance Indicators

| Pre-K-2 | 3–5 | 6–8 | 9–12 |
|---|---|---|---|
| | | 5.8.1. identify circumstances that can help or hinder healthy decision making. | 5.12.1. examine barriers that can hinder healthy decision making. |
| 5.2.1. identify situations when a health-related decision is needed. | 5.5.1. identify health-related situations that might require a thoughtful decision. | 5.8.2. determine when health-related situations require the application of a thoughtful decision-making process. | 5.12.2. determine the value of applying a thoughtful decision-making process in health related situations. |
| 5.2.2. differentiate between situations when a health-related decision can be made individually or when assistance is needed. | 5.5.2. analyze when assistance is needed when making a health-related decision. | 5.8.3. distinguish when individual or collaborative decision making is appropriate. | 5.12.3. justify when individual or collaborative decision making is appropriate. |
| | 5.5.3. list healthy options to health-related issues or problems. | 5.8.4. distinguish between healthy and unhealthy alternatives to health-related issues or problems. | 5.12.4. generate alternatives to health-related issues or problems. |
| | 5.5.4. predict the potential outcomes of each option when making a health-related decision. | 5.8.5. predict the potential short-term impact of each alternative on self and others. | 5.12.5. predict the potential short and long-term impact of each alternative on self and others. |
| | 5.5.5. choose a healthy option when making a decision. | 5.8.6. choose healthy alternatives over unhealthy alternatives when making a decision. | 5.12.6. defend the healthy choice when making decisions. |
| | 5.5.6. describe the outcomes of a health-related decision. | 5.8.7. analyze the outcomes of a health-related decision. | 5.12.7. evaluate the effectiveness of health-related decisions. |

**HEALTH EDUCATION STANDARD 6—Students will demonstrate the ability to use goal-setting skills to enhance health.**

## Rationale

Goal-setting skills ate essential to help students identify, adopt and maintain healthy behaviors. This standard includes the critical steps needed to achieve both short-term and long-term health goals. These skills make it possible for individuals to have aspirations and plans for the future.

## Performance Indicators

| Pre-K-2 | 3–5 | 6–8 | 9–12 |
|---|---|---|---|
| | | 6.8.1. assess personal health practices. | 6.12.1. assess personal health practices and overall health status. |
| 6.2.1. identify a short-term personal health goal and take action toward achieving the goal. | 6.5.1. set a personal health goal and track progress toward its achievement. | 6.8.2. develop a goal to adopt, maintain, or improve a personal health practice. | 6.12.2. develop a plan to attain a personal health goal that addresses strengths, needs, and risks. |
| 6.2.2. identify who can help when assistance is needed to achieve a personal health goal. | 6.5.2. identify resources to assist in achieving a personal health goal. | 6.8.3. apply strategies and skills needed to attain a personal health goal. | 6.12.3. implement strategies and monitor progress in achieving a personal health goal. |
| | | 6.8.4. describe how personal health goals can vary with changing abilities, priorities, and responsibilities. | 6.12.4. formulate an effective long-term personal health plan. |

**HEALTH EDUCATION STANDARD 7—Students will demonstrate the ability to practice health-enhancing behaviors and avoid or reduce health risks.**

## Rationale

Research confirms that practicing health enhancing behaviors can contribute to a positive quality of life. In addition, many diseases and injuries can be prevented by reducing harmful and risk taking behaviors. This standard promotes accepting personal responsibility for health and encourages the practice of healthy behaviors.

## Performance Indicators

| Pre-K-2 | 3–5 | 6–8 | 9–12 |
|---|---|---|---|
| | 7.5.1. identify responsible personal health behaviors. | 7.8.1. explain the importance of assuming responsibility for personal health behaviors. | 7.12.1. analyze the role of individual responsibility for enhancing health. |
| 7.2.1. demonstrate healthy practices and behaviors to maintain or improve personal health. | 7.5.2. demonstrate a variety of healthy practices and behaviors to maintain or improve personal health. | 7.8.2. demonstrate healthy practices and behaviors that will maintain or improve the health of self and others. | 7.12.2. demonstrate a variety of healthy practices and behaviors that will maintain or improve the health of self and others. |
| 7.2.2. demonstrate behaviors to avoid or reduce health risks. | 7.5.3. demonstrate a variety of behaviors to avoid or reduce health risks. | 7.8.3. demonstrate behaviors to avoid or reduce health risks to self and others. | 7.12.3. demonstrate a variety of behaviors to avoid or reduce health risks to self and others. |

**HEALTH EDUCATION STANDARD 8—Students will demonstrate the ability to advocate for personal, family and community health.**

## Rationale

Advocacy skills help students promote healthy norms and healthy behaviors. This standard helps students develop important skills to target their health enhancing messages and to encourage others to adopt healthy behaviors.

## Performance Indicators

| Pre-K-2 | 3–5 | 6–8 | 9–12 |
|---|---|---|---|
| 8.2.1. make requests to promote personal health. | 8.5.1. express opinions and give accurate information about health issues. | 8.8.1. state a health enhancing position on a topic and support it with accurate information. | 8.12.1. utilize accurate peer and societal norms to formulate a health-enhancing message. |
| 8.2.2. encourage peers to make positive health choices. | 8.5.2. encourage others to make positive health choices. | 8.8.2. demonstrate how to influence and support others to make positive health choices. | 8.12.2. demonstrate how to influence and support others to make positive health choices. |
| | | 8.8.3. work cooperatively to advocate for healthy individuals, families, and schools. | 8.12.3. work cooperatively as an advocate for improving personal, family and community health. |
| | | 8.8.4. identify ways that health messages and communication techniques can be altered for different audiences. | 8.12.4. adapt health messages and communication techniques to a specific target audience. |

**"Cited from Pre-publication document of National Health Education Standards, PreK-12, American Cancer Society. December 2005—August 2006"**

*State of Iowa Core Curriculum*

# Grades K-2

## Health Literacy

Health literacy, considered a 21st Century theme by the Partnership for 21st Century Skills, is, "*the degree to which individuals have the capacity to obtain, process, and understand basic health information and services needed to make appropriate health decisions*" (Nielsen-Bohlman, 2004). A health literate person is able to make appropriate decisions about their health as he or she progresses through life, as health care changes, and as societal norms change. The benefits of being health literate influence the full range of life's activities—home, school, work, society and culture (Zarcadoolas, 2005).

Lack of physical activity and exercise, poor nutritional choices, increased violence, increased substance abuse and other high risk behaviors are serious threats to living a healthy, active life. The essential concepts and skill sets for health literacy provide a framework for building capacity among Iowa's students to think critically about the decisions that affect health status for themselves, their families and their communities. Learning the concepts will form the knowledge base for the development of attitudes and habits of mind that will lead students to take responsibility for their personal health status. This proactive approach will have profound effects on families and society.

The essential concepts reflect the belief that children need to assess media messages at young ages and then develop critical evaluation skills as they intellectually, emotionally and socially mature (Zarcadoolas, 2005). Children must also take an active role in accessing and appropriately using information which affects their health (Nutbeam, 2000, St. Leger, 2001). Therefore, it is important to integrate the essential concepts and skill sets for health literacy across content areas, providing relevant contexts, problem based and service learning experiences. This will provide students opportunities to practice systemic thinking and problem solving processes that will lead to the creative solutions and proactive policies necessary to enhance health status in an interconnected, global society.

## Essential Concepts And/Or Essential Skills

**1) Understand and use basic health concepts to enhance personal, family, and community health.**

Know and use concepts related to health promotion and disease prevention.

- Identify ways to be healthy.
- Recognize multiple dimensions of wellness.
- Describe how physical, emotional, social, and environmental factors influence personal health.
- Identify ways to prevent illness and injury.
- Know when and how to ask for help with health care.
- Identify the impact of personal health behaviors on the functioning of body systems.
- Recognize that personal health behaviors influence an individual's well being.
- List preventive physical and mental health measures, including proper diet, nutrition, exercise, risk avoidance and stress reduction.

Analyze influencing factors on health enhancing behaviors.

- Identify positive and negative effects of media and technology upon health practices and choices.

| Quadrant C | Quadrant D |
|---|---|
| Working in cooperative groups, students will create a list of responses to stressful life events. Students will distinguish between positive and negative stress management strategies. Each small group will develop skits that model positive stress management strategies to share with classmates. | Each student will interview family members about stress management strategies that are typically practiced. Students will develop a communication tool (ie: brochure, poster, flier, etc.) that could be posted at home to remind family members of positive stress management strategies. |
| **Quadrant A** | **Quadrant B** |
| Students will view and discuss a teacher demonstration explaining the concept of stress. | As a class students will discuss personal stressors and strategies for managing personal stress. |

**2) Understand and use interactive literacy and social skills to enhance personal, family, and community health.**

Demonstrate social and communication skills to enhance health and increase safety.

- Demonstrate verbal and nonverbal ways to express wants, needs, and feelings appropriately.
- Choose effective conflict management strategies.
- Show how to ask for help.
- Identify ways to communicate care, consideration, empathy and respect for self and others.

Advocate for personal, family and community health.

- Identify personal health needs.
- Articulate ways to influence and support others to make positive health choices.
- Identify ways to improve family and community health.
- Recognize mean and violent acts and demonstrate appropriate responses.

**3) Recognize critical literacy/thinking skills related to personal, family and community wellness.**

Demonstrate decision making skills.

- Understand the interrelationships between decisions, choices and consequences.
- Recognize the effectiveness of health-related decisions.
- Recognize the need to ask for assistance when making health-related decisions.
- Identify that health related decisions have an impact on individual, family, community, and environment.

Demonstrate goal-setting skills.

- Set personal goals.

**4) Identify influences that affect personal health and the health of others.**

Analyze the influence of family, peers, health professionals, culture, media, technology, and other health factors.

- Identify negative and positive health practices.
- Describe how culture influences personal health choices.
- Identify trusted adults/professionals who can help.

Access valid information, products and services.

- Selects appropriate products for minor injuries or illnesses.

**5) Demonstrate behaviors that foster healthy, active lifestyles for individuals and the benefit of society.**

Achieve and maintain health enhancing level of physical activity.

- Practice fitness skills.
- Practice basic health enhancing physical behaviors.

Practice preventive health behaviors.

- Identify stress and stress relievers.
- Identify risk behaviors and practice healthy choices.
- Identify healthy foods.
- Identify behaviors that contribute to total wellness for individuals, families and communities

.

# Grades 3-5

## Health Literacy

Health literacy, considered a 21st Century theme by the Partnership for 21st Century Skills, is, "*the degree to which individuals have the capacity to obtain, process, and understand basic health information and services needed to make appropriate health decisions*" (Nielsen-Bohlman, 2004). A health literate person is able to make appropriate decisions about their health as he or she progresses through life, as health care changes, and as societal norms change. The benefits of being health literate influence the full range of life's activities—home, school, work, society and culture (Zarcadoolas, 2005).

Lack of physical activity and exercise, poor nutritional choices, increased violence, increased substance abuse and other high risk behaviors are serious threats to living a healthy, active life. The essential concepts and skill sets for health literacy provide a framework for building capacity among Iowa's students to think critically about the decisions that affect health status for themselves, their families and their communities. Learning the concepts will form the knowledge base for the development of attitudes and habits of mind that will lead students to take responsibility for their personal health status. This proactive approach will have profound effects on families and society.

The essential concepts reflect the belief that children need to assess media messages at young ages and then develop critical evaluation skills as they intellectually, emotionally and socially mature (Zarcadoolas, 2005). Children must also take an active role in accessing and appropriately using information which affects their health (Nutbeam, 2000, St. Leger, 2001). Therefore, it is important to integrate the essential concepts and skill sets for health literacy across content areas, providing relevant contexts, problem based and service learning experiences. This will provide students opportunities to practice systemic thinking and problem solving processes that will lead to the creative solutions and proactive policies necessary to enhance health status in an interconnected, global society.

## Essential Concepts And/Or Essential Skills

**1) Obtain, interpret, understand and use basis health concepts to enhance personal, family, and community health.**

Know and use concepts related to health promotion and disease prevention.

- Describe the influence of risk and protective factors.
- Identify examples of physical, emotional, intellectual, environmental, social, sexual and spiritual wellness during childhood.
- Analyze how heredity, environment and personal health are related.
- Explain proper prevention/management of health crises.
- Identify where to find help with health care when needed.
- Describe the impact of personal health behaviors on the functioning of body systems.
- Identify how personal choices impact health and disease prevention.
- Describe preventive physical and mental health measures, including proper diet, nutrition, exercise, risk avoidance and stress reduction.

Analyze influencing factors on health enhancing behaviors.

- Describe how diverse families, peers, cultural practices and attitudes influence health related decisions.
- Describe how media, technology, research and medical advances impact health.
- Recognize how national and international public health and safety issues affect personal and family health status.

**2) Utilize interactive literacy and social skills to establish personal family, and community health goals.**

Demonstrate social and communication skills that enhance health and increase safety.

- Demonstrate appropriate verbal and nonverbal communication skills to enhance health of self and others.
- Practice strategies to manage or resolve conflict.
- State methods of obtaining help for self and others.
- Demonstrate ways to communicate care, consideration, empathy and respect for self and others.

Advocate for personal, family and community health.

- Identify personal, family and community health needs.
- Demonstrate how to influence and support others to make positive health choices.
- Describe ways to improve family and community health.
- Articulate effective communication related to health care practices.
- Use assertive communications skills to consistently advocate for a healthy, violence-free environment.

| Quadrant C | Quadrant D |
|---|---|
| The students will work in cooperative groups to create "conflict" scenarios. The students will develop a script for the scenario that demonstrates the steps of conflict resolution. The student will videotape the scripted conflicts to share with other classes. | Students will serve as trained conflict managers for younger students, modeling the resolution process and guiding younger students to an agreeable solution. |
| Quadrant A | Quadrant B |
| The students will discuss the specific steps of conflict resolution. | Working in small groups, the students will demonstrate knowledge of conflict resolution strategies by role-playing teacher created scenarios based upon playground and principal referrals. |

### 3) Demonstrate critical literacy/thinking skills related to personal, family, and community wellness.

Demonstrate decision making skills.

- Explain different approaches to making decisions.
- Describe the effectiveness of health-related decisions.
- Demonstrate the ability to seek assistance when making health related decisions.
- Recognize that health related decisions have an impact on individual, family, community, and environment.

Demonstrate goal-setting skills.

- Develop goals to enhance health status.

### 4) Recognize that media and other influences affect personal, family and community health.

Analyze the influence of family, peers, health professionals, culture, media, technology, and other health factors.

- Demonstrate appropriate responses to negative and positive health influences.
- Recognize public health policies that aid in the prevention and maintenance of school and community health.
- Describe the influence of cultural diversities on health behaviors.
- Explain how information from school and family influences health.
- Identify characteristics of valid health information sources.
- Recognize the techniques used by print and non-print media sources.

Access valid information, products and services.

- Identify factors that influence the selection of health, products and services.

### 5) Demonstrate behaviors that foster healthy, active lifestyles for individuals and the benefit of society.

Achieve and maintain health enhancing level of physical activity.

- Identify personal physical strengths and weaknesses.
- Engage in physical activities to improve fitness components.

Practice preventive health behaviors.

- Demonstrate appropriate and effective stress management.
- Assess risk factors that contribute to healthy choices.
- Choose healthy foods.
- Demonstrate behaviors that contribute to holistic wellness for individuals, families and communities.

# Grades 6-8

## Health Literacy

Health literacy, considered a 21st Century theme by the Partnership for 21st Century Skills, is, *"the degree to which individuals have the capacity to obtain, process, and understand basic heal A information and services needed to make appropriate health decisions"* (Nielsen-Bohlman, 2004). A health literate person is able to make appropriate decisions about their health as he or she progresses through life, as health care changes, and as societal norms change. The benefits of being health literate influence the full range of life's activities—home, school, work, society and culture (Zarcadoolas, 2005).

Lack of physical activity and exercise, poor nutritional choices, increased violence, increased substance abuse and other high risk behaviors are serious threats to living a healthy, active life. The essential concepts and skill sets for health literacy provide a framework for building capacity among Iowa's students to think critically about the decisions that affect health status for themselves, their families and their communities. Learning the concepts will form the knowledge base for the development of attitudes and habits of mind that will lead students to take responsibility for their personal health status. This proactive approach will have profound effects on families and society.

The essential concepts reflect the belief that children need to assess media messages at young ages and then develop critical evaluation skills as they intellectually, emotionally and socially mature (Zarcadoolas, 2005). Children must also take an active role in accessing and appropriately using information which affects their health (Nutbeam, 2000, St. Leger, 2001). Therefore, it is important to integrate the essential concepts and skill sets for health literacy across content areas, providing relevant contexts, problem based and service learning experiences. This will provide students opportunities to practice systemic thinking and problem solving processes that will lead to the creative solutions and proactive policies necessary to enhance health status in an interconnected, global society.

## Essential Concepts And/Or Essential Skills

**1) Demonstrate functional health literacy skills to obtain, interpret, understand and use basic health concepts to enhance personal, family and community health.**

Know and use concepts related to health promotion and disease prevention.

- Anticipate the influence of risk and protective factors.
- Describe the interrelationships of the wellness dimensions: physical, emotional, intellectual, environmental, social, sexual and spiritual wellness during adolescence.
- Evaluate the impact of genetics/family history with personal health decisions.
- Demonstrate skills necessary for proper prevention/management of health crises, i.e. injury, depression, chronic illness.
- Explain how appropriate health care can promote personal health.
- Recognize prevention and control of health problems are influenced by research and medical advances.
- Recognize the historical impact of disease and other health problems.
- Evaluate the impact of personal health behaviors on the functioning of body systems.
- Develop healthy personal choices to promote health maintenance and disease prevention.
- Develop preventive physical and mental health measures, including proper diet, nutrition, exercise, risk avoidance and stress reduction.

Analyze influencing factors on health enhancing behaviors.

- Describe how diverse families, peers, cultural practices and attitudes influence health.
- Articulate how media, technology, research and medical advances impact health.
- Articulate how national and international public health and safety issues affect personal and family health status.

**2) Utilize interactive literacy and social skills to establish personal, family, and community health goals.**

Demonstrate social and communication skills to enhance health and increase safety.

- Apply appropriate communication skills to enhance health of self and others.
- Utilize effective conflict management strategies.
- Demonstrate proper methods of obtaining help for self and others.
- Generate ways to communicate care, consideration, empathy and respect for self and others.

Advocate for personal, family and community health.

- Develop a health message to meet the health needs of a target audience.
- Model how to influence and support others to make positive health choices.
- Collaborate to improve family and community health.
- Articulate effective communication methods to accurately express health information and ideas.
- Recognize media and legislative advocacy efforts to promote positive health for self and others.
- Identify power structures that support advocacy of a healthy, violence-free environment.

### 3) Apply critical literacy/thinking skills related to personal, family and community wellness.

Demonstrate decision making skills.

- Apply skills needed to make healthy decisions.
- Analyze the effectiveness of health-related decisions.
- Describe the ethical factors that influence health related decisions.
- Integrate the roles of individual, family, community and cultures when making health related decisions.
- Demonstrate how health related decisions impact individual, family, community and environment.

Demonstrate goal setting skills.

- Implement goals to enhance personal health and track its achievement.

### 4) Employ media literacy skills to analyze media and other influences to effectively manage personal, family and community health situations.

Analyze the influence of family, peers, health professionals, culture, media, technology, and other health factors.

- Demonstrate appropriate responses to negative and positive health influences.
- Discuss the role of public health policies in prevention and maintenance of school and community health.
- Determine how cultural diversities enrich and challenge health behaviors.
- Analyze how information influences health.
- Determine reliability, accuracy, dependability of health information sources.
- Describe the techniques used by print and non-print media sources.

Access valid information, products and services.

- Differentiate factors that influence the selection of health products and services.
- Not applicable.

| Quadrant C | Quadrant D |
|---|---|
| The student will select one print advertisement or commercial that encourages unhealthy behavior. S(He) will compose a letter to the company that produces the product promoted in the ad. The letter will minimally include a justification of three reasons to request the ad or commercial be taken off the market. | Each student will create either a health related print advertisement or commercial utilizing at least one advertisement technique. The ad or commercial must encourage middle school students to engage in a health enhancing behavior. Ads will be posted throughout the school and commercials viewed during homeroom and shared with elementary classes. |
| **Quadrant A** | **Quadrant B** |
| The student will be provided materials to view and define print examples of various media techniques used to influence consumers. | Student will bring a favorite magazine to critique health related magazine advertisements and commercials. The students will consider the following criteria:<br><br>• Describe the ad/commercial<br>• State the advertising technique(s) used<br>• Identify the target audience<br>• Discuss the effectiveness of the ad/commercial |

### 5) Demonstrate behaviors that foster healthy, active lifestyles for individuals and the benefit of society.

Achieve and maintain health enhancing level of physical activity.

- Develop, implement and evaluate goals for physical health.
- Engage in activities to improve cardio-vascular and muscular strength and endurance, flexibility, and body composition.

Practice preventive health behaviors.

- Practice appropriate and effective stress management.
- Analyze risk factors and make healthy choices.
- Implement a plan reflecting healthy food choices.
- Implement behaviors that contribute to holistic wellness for individuals, families and communities.

# What Is Wellness?

A quick Internet search for a definition of wellness will, literally, give you thousands of answers. The Merriam-Webster Dictionary lists the following:

The quality or state of being in good health especially as an actively sought goal.

The World Health Organization considers wellness to be "a state of complete physical, mental, and social well-being and not merely the absence of disease or infirmity."

What is consistent throughout all of the various definitions is that wellness is multi-dimensional and involves working toward a positive state of well-being. Most note that it is not only physical but also mental and emotional.

Physical Wellness—involves exercise, knowledge of nutrition, and responsible, informed decision making about a variety of behaviors from safety to sleep. Seeking appropriate medical care, when needed, is also considered part of physical wellness.

Mental Wellness—is the engaging of the mind in learning, problem-solving, critical thinking, and creativity. It is keeping the mind active and stimulated.

Emotional Wellness—is the ability to understand and accept your feelings, the capacity to adjust to change, and knowing how to cope with stress in a positive way. It also involves the ability to be introspective about behaviors and actions.

Other areas of wellness that are included in some of the models are:

Social—
Financial—
Spiritual—
Occupational—
Environmental—

## Children and Wellness

The definition of wellness does not change for children. The role of the teacher is two-fold. It is to educate students about the various components within each dimension and to provide them with an environment where they can strive toward a sense of physical, mental, and emotional well-being.

## Education

There are several ways to provide information on wellness. Classroom teachers can teach entire health lessons on topics such as safety, bones and muscles, nutrition, and feelings. They can also do cross-curricular activities. When teaching a math lesson on addition, use caloric numbers of fast food items from local chains so that students understand how much they are eating. In language arts, reading a book about bullying can be followed by a class discussion on emotional wellness. Topics such as heart rate and the effects of exercise can be carried over into physical education class. Finally, the teacher should provide students with the names of quality resources and explain how to sort through the vast amount of material that is now available to find reliable and dependable information.

## Environmental

The classroom, itself, can help students develop wellness. Lessons and activities need to be engaging for the students and allow for thinking and creativity. It should be a positive, safe place where a student can feel a sense of belonging. Student work can be displayed around the room. Seating arrangements can be made to enhance peer interactions. The teacher can also make sure that students are involved in some decision making, such as creating classroom rules, and that they learn to accept the consequences of their actions and behaviors.

A child who is working on their wellness, along with all of the other areas of curriculum, is a child who is learning to become a positive, productive, and valuable member of society.

# How Can We Strengthen Children's Self-Esteem?

Lilian Katz

Most parents want their young children to have a healthy sense of self-esteem. That desire can also be seen in education–schools around the country include self-esteem among their goals. Many observers believe that low self-esteem lies at the bottom of many of society's problems.

Even though self-esteem has been studied far more than 100 years, specialists and educators continue to debate its precise nature and development. Nevertheless, they generally agree that parents and other adults who are important to children play a major role in laying a solid foundation for a child's development.

## What Is Self-Esteem?

When parents and teachers of young children talk about the need for good self-esteem, they usually mean that children should have "good feelings" about themselves. With young children, self-esteem refers to the extent to which they expect to be accepted and valued by the adults and peers who are important to them.

Children with a healthy sense of self-esteem feel that the important adults in their lives accept them, care about them, and would go out of their way to ensure that they are safe and well. They feel that those adults would be upset if anything happened to them and would miss them if they were separated. Children with low self-esteem, on the other hand, feel that the important adults and peers in their lives do not accept them, do not care about them very much, and would not go out of their way to ensure their safety and well-being.

During their early years, young children's self-esteem is based largely on their perceptions of how the important adults in their lives judge them. The extent to which children believe they have the characteristics valued by the important adults and peers in their lives figures greatly in the development of self-esteem. For example, in families and communities that value athletic ability highly, children who excel in athletics are likely to have a high level of self-esteem, whereas children who are less athletic or who are criticized as being physically inept or clumsy are likely to suffer from low self-esteem.

Families, communities, and ethnic and cultural groups vary in the criteria on which self-esteem is based. For example, some groups may emphasize physical appearance, and some may evaluate boys and girls differently. Stereotyping, prejudice, and discrimination are also factors that may contribute to low self-esteem among children.

## How Can We Help Children Develop a Healthy Sense of Self-Esteem?

The foundations of self-esteem are laid early in life when infants develop attachments with the adults who are responsible for them. When adults readily respond to their cries and smiles, babies learn to feel loved and valued. Children come to feel loved and accepted by being loved and accepted by people they look up to. As young children learn to trust their parents and others who care for them to satisfy their basic needs, they gradually feel wanted, valued, and loved.

Self-esteem is also related to children's feelings of belonging to a group and being able to adequately function in their group. When toddlers become preschoolers, for example, they are expected to control their impulses and adopt the rules of the family and community in which they are growing. Successfully adjusting to these groups helps to strengthen feelings of belonging to them.

Written by Lilian Katz, Director of the ERIC Clearinghouse on Elementary and Early Childhood Education.

One point to make is that young children are unlikely to have their self-esteem strengthened from excessive praise or flattery. On the contrary, it may raise some doubts in children; many children can see through flattery and may even dismiss an adult who heaps on praise as a poor source of support–one who is not very believable.

The following points may be helpful in strengthening and supporting a healthy sense of self-esteem in your child:

**As they grow, children become increasingly sensitive to the evaluations of their peers.** You and your child's teachers can help your child learn to build healthy relationships with his or her peers.

**When children develop stronger ties with their peers in school or around the neighborhood, they may begin to evaluate themselves differently from the way they were taught at home.** You can help your child by being clear about your own values and keeping the lines of communication open about experiences outside the home.

**Children do not acquire self-esteem at once nor do they always feel good about themselves in every situation.** A child may feel self-confident and accepted at home but not around the neighborhood or in a preschool class. Furthermore, as children interact with their peers or learn to function in school or some other place, they may feel accepted and liked one moment and feel different the next You can help in these instances by reassuring your child that you support and accept him or her even while others do not.

**A child's sense of self-worth is more likely to deepen when adults respond to the child's interests and efforts with appreciation rather than just praise.** For example, if your child shows interest in something you are doing, you might include the child in the activity. Or if the child shows interest in an animal in the garden, you might help the child find more information about it. In this way, you respond positively to your child's interest by treating it seriously. Flattery and praise, on the contrary, distract children from the topics they are interested in. Children may develop a habit of showing interest in a topic just to receive flattery.

**Young children are more likely to benefit from tasks and activities that offer a real challenge than from those that are merely frivolous or fun.** For example, you can involve your child in chores around the house, such as preparing meals or caring for pets, that stretch his or her abilities and give your child a sense of accomplishment.

**Self-esteem is most likely to be fostered when children are esteemed by the adults who are important to them.** To esteem children means to treat them respectfully, ask their views and opinions, take their views and opinions seriously, and give them meaningful and realistic feedback.

**You can help your child develop and maintain healthy self-esteem by helping him or her cope with defeats, rather than emphasizing constant successes and triumphs.** During times of disappointment or crisis, your child's weakened self-esteem can be strengthened when you let me child know that your love and support remain unchanged. When the crisis has passed, you can help your child reflect on what went wrong. The next time a crisis occurs, your child can use the knowledge gained from overcoming past difficulties to help cope with a new crisis. A child's sense of self-worth and self-confidence is not likely to deepen when adults deny that life has its ups and downs.

## Conclusion

Parents can play an important role in strengthening children's self-esteem by treating them respectfully, taking their views and opinions seriously, and expressing appreciation to them. Above all, parents must keep in mind that self-esteem is an important part of every child's development.

## Where Can I Get More Information?

The ERIC Clearinghouse on Elementary and Early Childhood Education can provide more information on strengthening self-esteem among children:

ERIC Clearinghouse on Elementary and Early Childhood Education University of Illinois 805 West Pennsylvania Avenue Urbana. II. 61801-4897 1-800-583-4135

## Source

Most of the following references–those identified with an ED or EJ number–have been abstracted and are in the ERIC database. Documents with an ED number can be found on microfiche at more than 900 locations or can be ordered in paper copy from the ERIC Document Reproduction Service at 1-800-443- ERIC. The journal articles can be found at most research libraries. Call 1-800-LET-ERIC for more details.

Amundson, K. 1991. *101 Ways Parents Can Help Students Achieve.* Arlington, VA: American Association of School Administrators.

Cutright, M. C. February 1992. "Self-Esteem: The Key to a Child's Success and Happiness." *PTA Today* 17 (4): 5–6.

Dusa, G. S. February 1992. "15 Ways Parents Can Boost Self-Esteem." *Learning* 20 (6): 26–27.

Isenberg, J., and N.L. Quisenberry. February 1988. "Play: A Necessity for All Children." A position paper of the Association for Childhood Education International (ACEI). *Childhood Education* 64 (3): 138–145. EJ 367 943.

Katz, L.G. 1993. *Distinctions Between Self-Esteem and Narcissism: Implications for Practice.* Urbana, IL: ERIC Clearinghouse an Elementary and Early Childhood Education. ED 363 452.

Katz, L.G., and S.C. Chard. 1989. *Engaging Children's Minds: The Project Approach.* Norwood, NJ: Ablex. ED 326 302.

Kramer, P. April 1992. "Fostering Self-Esteem Can Keep Kids Safe and Sound." *PTA Today* 17 (6): 10–11.

Markus, H.R., and S. Kitayama. 1991. "Culture and the Self: Implications for Cognition. Emotions, and Motivation." *Psychological Review* 98 (2): 224–253.

McDaniel, S. April 1986. "Political Priority #1: Teaching Kids To Like Themselves." *New Options* 27: 1.

National Association of Elementary School Principals. 1990. Early Childhood Education and the Elementary School Principal: Standards for Quality Programs for Young Children. Alexandria, VA: NAESP.

National Association of Elementary School Principals. 1991. The Little Things Make a Big Difference: How To Help Your Children Succeed in School. Alexandria VA: NAESP.

Popkin, Michael, H. 1993. Active Parenting Today: For Parents of 2 to 12 Year Olds. Parent's Guide. Marietta, GA: Active Parenting Publishers.

## Credits

Written by Lilian Katz, Director of the ERIC Clearinghouse on Elementary and Early Childhood Education.

This publication was prepared by ACCESS ERIC in association with the ERIC Clearinghouse on Elementary and Early Childhood Education, with funding from the Office of Educational Research and Improvement, U.S. Department of Education, under Contract No. RR92024001. The opinions expressed in this brochure do not necessarily reflect the positions or policies of the U.S. Department of Education.

## Early Years are Learning Years. Self-Esteem and Young Children: You are the Key

**National Association for the Education of Young Children 1998**

It's been known for more than 100 years that a child's emotional life strongly influences his interpersonal relations, behavior, and learning. Recent research underscores the importance of the early childhood years as a critically important period for the development of future mental health and self-esteem. Children with a healthy sense of self-esteem feel that the important adults in their lives love them, accept them, and would go out of their way to ensure their safety and well-being. Low self-esteem (feeling unwanted, unloved, and unaccepted) can often lead to learning disabilities, disciplinary problems, and depression later in life. Following are some essential elements for what young children need for healthy emotional development.

*From Early Years are Learning Years. Self-Esteem and Young Children: You are the Key.* Copyright © 1998. Reprinted with permission from the National Association for the Education of Young Children.

### Commitment

Every child needs at least one reliable, responsive adult who is connected to and available to them for the long term. Without this, children are unlikely to learn to trust, or suffering the anguish of broken trust, learn not to trust again. This creates permanent damage in their ability to develop productive relationships, possibly including relationships with child care professionals and teachers. In addition, a child who lacks an adult to count on and to comfort her doesn't feel lovable and may not behave "lovably." Because she has never experienced and absorbed compassion, she has none to give. A warm and caring adult can sometimes tip the balance between a child who learns and a child who learns to fail.

### Communication

Communication is the vehicle for intellectual development, exchanging information, sharing feelings, and developing strong emotional bonds. A parent or family member who chats encouragingly with a child about many of the things he's doing, thinking, and feeling enhances the child's language development, and helps him build confidence in his independence.

### Boundaries

Reasonable and reasonably consistent limits help a child feel safe, feel like a good person, and feel likable. Usually, a child will not strive to meet the standards set by adults, will not curb her urgent impulses, and will not bother to make the extra effort, unless those standards are achievable for her developmental stage, she understands the limits, and she likes and respects the adult.

### Appreciation

A child's sense of self-worth is more likely to deepen when adults respond to the child's interests and efforts with appreciation rather than just praise. Excessive praise or flattery may raise doubts in children, and many will dismiss an adult who heaps on praise as one who is not very believable.

### Coping Strategies

You can help a child develop and maintain healthy self-esteem by helping him cope with difficult situations. Coping strategies include sharing, managing anger, resolving conflict, and dealing with stress During times of disappointment or crisis, a child's weakened self-esteem can be strengthened if you let her know that your love and support remain unchanged. When the crisis has passed, you can help the child reflect on what went wrong. The next time a crisis occurs, she can use the knowledge gained from overcoming past difficulties.

### Modeling

Essential for social learning, positive, competent, and effective role models teach children about the importance of becoming productive and caring individuals.

It takes time to nurture children. They require lots of leisurely time with loved ones and with others who enjoy them. Parents, child care professionals, and teachers can play an important role in strengthening children's self-esteem by treating them respectfully, taking their views and opinions seriously, and expressing appreciation to them.

## Additional Resources

Greenberg, P. 1998. "Some Thoughts about Phonics, Feelings, Don Quixote, Diversity, and Democracy: Teaching Young Children to Read. Write, and Spell." *Young Children* 53 (4).

ERIC Clearinghouse on Elementary and Early Childhood Education. http://ericeece.org, http://npin.org

## Self-compassion

Self-compassion is extending compassion to one's self in instances of perceived inadequacy, failure, or general suffering. Dr. Kristin Neff has defined self-compassion as being of three main components—self-kindness, common humanity, and mindfulness.

Self-kindness: Self-compassion entails being warm toward oneself when encountering pain and personal shortcomings, rather than ignoring them or hurting oneself with self-criticism.

Common humanity: Self-compassion also involves recognizing that suffering and personal failure is part of the shared human experience.

Mindfulness: Self-compassion requires taking a balanced approach to one's negative emotions so that feelings are neither suppressed nor exaggerated. Negative thoughts are observed with openness, so that they are held in mindful awareness. Mindfulness is a non-judgmental, receptive mind state in which individuals observe their thoughts and feelings as they are, without trying to suppress or deny them.

It appears that self-compassion offers the same mental health benefits as self-esteem, but with fewer of its drawbacks such as narcissism, ego-defensive anger, inaccurate self-perceptions, self-worthy contingency, or social comparison.

Neff, K.D. (2003a). "The development and validation of a scale to measure self-compassion". Self and Identity 2 (3): 223-250. doi: 10.1080/15298860309027 (https://dx.doi.org/10.1080%2F15298860309027).

Brown, K.W.; Ryan, R.M. (2003). "The benefits of being present: Mindfulness and its role in the psychological well-being". *Journal of Personality and Social Psychology* **84** (4): 822-848. doi: 10.1037/0022-3514.84.4.822 (https://dx.doi.org/10.1037%2F0022-3514.84.4.822). PMID 12703651 (https://www.ncbi.nlm.nih.gov/pubmed/12703651).

Leary, M R.; Tate, E.B.; Adams, C.E.; Allen, A.B.; Handcock, J. (2007). "Self-compassion and reactions to unpleasant self-relevant events. The implications of treating oneself kindly". *Journal of Personality and Social Psychology* **92** (5): 887-904. doi: 10.1037/0022-3514.92.5.887 (https://dx.doi.org/10.1037%2F0022-3514.92.5.887). PMID 17484611 (https://www.ncbi.nlm.nih.gov/pubmed/17494611).

# Bullying

**Definitions:**
- A form of abuse and harassment perpetrated by a person or group of people who are physically or socially more powerful than a weaker peer.
- An act of repeated, intentional aggressive behavior intended to physically hurt another person and/or inflict mental or emotional distress. Can be emotional, verbal, and/or physical. Can also involve threats of worse abuse if the victim "tells."

Can include name calling, the silent treatment, arguing others into submission, manipulation, false gossip, lies, false rumors, staring, giggling, laughing, mocking, acts of degradation, physical abuse.

**Characteristics of a student who bullies in elementary school:**

- Is older than the victim
- Is usually more popular with peers than victim
- Has low self-esteem
- Exhibits aggressive behavior
- Lacks a moral compass
- Relationships with friends and/or parents marked by conflict (may be or have been a victim)

**Characteristics of a student who is bullied:**

- Boys or girls
- Loses interest in school—grades drop—high absenteeism
- Depressed or withdrawn
- Difficulty sleeping
- May have unexplained injuries or bruises

**Effects on a student who is bullied:**

- Poor performance in school
- Isolation, loneliness
- Depression
- Anxiety

- Low self-esteem
- Increased illness
- Suicide
- Becoming a bully
- Violence toward school

**What to do:**

Teachers

- Be alert and perceptive—ACT
- Create a safe classroom—zero tolerance
- Have class discussion about positive interactions with peers and bullying
- Teach and model empathy and acceptance of diversity
- Develop, with student input, rules regarding bullying
- Encourage reporting of bullying
- Praise positive behavior and avoidance of bullying
- Teach conflict-resolution and anger management skills
- Do role-playing exercises

Schools-
- Discussions/information sessions/training on all aspects of bullying
- Involve all school personal
- Develop schoolwide, anti-bullying policy
- Increase adult supervision in hallways, during recess, etc.
- Involve parents in education and prevention programs

## Federal Laws

Although no federal law directly addresses bullying, in some cases, bullying overlaps with discriminatory harassment when it is based on race, national origin, color, sex, age, disability, or religion. When bullying and harassment overlap, federally-funded schools (including colleges and universities) have an obligation to resolve the harassment. When the situation is not adequately resolved, the U.S. Department of Education's Office for Civil Rights and the U.S. Department of Justice's Civil Rights Division may be able to help.

## Are there federal laws that apply to bullying?

At present, no federal law directly addresses bullying. In some cases, bullying overlaps with discriminatory harassment which is covered under federal civil rights laws enforced by the U.S. Department of Education (ED) and the U.S. Department of Justice (DOJ). No matter what label is used (e.g., bullying, hazing, teasing), schools are obligated by these laws to address conduct that is:

- Severe, pervasive or persistent
- Creates a hostile environment at school. That is, it is sufficiently serious that it interferes with or limits a student's ability to participate in or benefit from the services, activities, or opportunities offered by a school
- Based on a student's race, color, national origin, sex, disability, or religion*
  - Although the US Department of Education, under Title VI of the Civil Rights Act of 1964 does not directly cover religion, often religious based harassment is based on shared ancestry of ethnic characteristics which is covered. The US Department of Justice has jurisdiction over religion under Title IV of the Civil Rights Act of 1964.

## What are the federal civil rights laws ED and DOJ enforce?

- A school that fails to respond appropriately to harassment of students based on a protected class may be violating one or more civil rights laws enforced by the Department of Education and the Department of Justice, including:

- Title IV and Title VI of the Civil Rights Act of 1964
- Title IX of the Education Amendments of 1972
- Section 504 of the Rehabilitation Act of 1973
- Titles II and III of the Americans with Disabilities Act
- Individuals with Disabilities Education Act (IDEA)

## Do federal civil rights laws cover harassment of LGBT youth?

- Title IX and Title IV do not prohibit discrimination based solely on sexual orientation, but they protect all students, including students who are LGBT or perceived to be LGBT, from sex-based harassment.
- Harassment based on sex and sexual orientation are not mutually exclusive. When students are harassed based on their actual or perceived sexual orientation, they may also be subjected to forms of sex discrimination recognized under Title IX.

## What is an example of a case were harassment based on sex and sexual orientation overlap?

- A female high school student was spit on, slammed into lockers, mocked, and routinely called names because she did not conform to feminine stereotypes and because of her sexual orientation. The student had short hair, a deep voice, and wore male clothing. After the harassment started, she told some classmates she was a lesbian, and the harassment worsened. The school described the harassment as "sexual orientation harassment" in its incident reports and did not take any action.
- In this case, the student was harassed based on her non-conformity to gender stereotypes. In this case, then, although the school labeled the incident as "sexual orientation harassment," the harassment was also based on sex and covered under Title IX.

## What are a school's obligations regarding harassment based on protected classes?

Anyone can report harassing conduct to a school. When a school receives a complaint they must take certain steps to investigate and resolve the situation.

- Immediate and appropriate action to investigate or otherwise determine what happened.
- Inquiry must be prompt, thorough, and impartial.
- Interview targeted students, offending students, and witnesses, and maintain written documentation of investigation
- Communicate with targeted students regarding steps taken to end harassment
- Check in with targeted students to ensure that harassment has ceased
- When an investigation reveals that harassment has occurred, a school should take steps reasonably calculated to:
- End the harassment,
- Eliminate any hostile environment,
- Prevent harassment from recurring, and
- Prevent retaliation against the targeted student(s) or complainant(s).

## What should a school do to resolve a harassment complaint?

- Appropriate responses will depend on the facts of each case.
- School must be an active participant in responding to harassment and should take reasonable steps when crafting remedies to minimize burdens on the targeted students.
- Possible responses include:
  - Develop, revise, and publicize:
    - Policy prohibiting harassment and discrimination
    - Grievance procedures for students to file harassment complaints
    - contact information for Title IX/Section 504/Title VI coordinators
  - Implement training for staff and administration on identifying and addressing harassment
  - Provide monitors or additional adult supervision in areas where harassment occurs

- Determine consequences and services for harassers, including whether discipline is appropriate
- Limit interactions between harassers and targets
- Provide harassed student an additional opportunity to obtain a benefit that was denied (e.g., retaking a test/class).
- Provide services to a student who was denied a benefit (e.g., academic support services).

## Are there resources for schools to assist with resolving harassment complaints?

The Department of Justice's Community Relations Service is the Department's "peacemaker" for community conflicts and tensions arising from differences of race, color and national origin and to prevent and respond to violent hate crimes committed on the basis of: gender, gender identity, sexual orientation, religion, disability, race, color, and national origin. It is a free, impartial, confidential and voluntary Federal Agency that offers mediation, conciliation, technical assistance, and training.

## What if the harassment continues?

If harassment persists, consider filing a formal grievance with the district and contacting the U.S. Department of Education's Office for Civil Rights and from the U.S. Department of Justice's Civil Rights Division.

## State Laws

BullyPolice.org – A watch-dog organization – Advocating for bullied children and Reporting on State Anti Bullying Laws. A State by State overview of bullying laws with comments about strenghts and weaknesses.

## Nutrition

## Current Status of Children's Health

- Estimated 16% to 25% of all school-aged children in the U.S. are overweight.
- Needs for key nutrients are not being met. Children are eating more but getting less-eating nutrient-deficient, high-calorie foods.
- Physical activity has continued to decrease in both school and in sports activities.
- Increase in rate of diabetes, high blood pressure, cholesterol, asthma, and allergies in children.

## Nutrition and Learning

Students who are well nourished:
1. Are more attentive
2. Have better behavior
3. Have better coordination skills
4. Are able to spend more time on task
5. Have a higher level of energy for learning
6. Have higher math/reading scores

## Nutrition Education Law

*Child Nutrition Reauthorization Healthy, Hunger-Free Kids Act (2010)*:
- More nutritious school meals
- More time allotted for physical education
- Nutrition education in schools
- A school district wellness policy

## Creating a Healthy School Environment

- Encourage breakfast-the most important meal of the day
- Model appropriate behavior-eat with students
            -eat school meals
            -drink milk at school
- Do not use food for rewards or school fundraisers
            -Alternatives
- Provide ideas for healthy snacks at parties and events
- Form a student health team to help create and maintain a healthy school environment

## Education

- Action for Healthy Kids

   National and State Organization, composed of experts from a wide variety of backgrounds (pediatrics, school boards, physical education, AFT, NEA, National Dairy Council, etc.)

   Provide education, support, and resources to promote a healthy school environment.

   www.actionforhealthykids.org

- National Dairy Council

  Free nutrition education materials and lesson plans for school teachers.
  www.midwestdairy.com

  -Think Your Drink
  -Serving Sizes
  -Combination Foods
  -Body Building Snacks and Meals
  -Food Groups
  -Healthy Breakfast
  -Food Labels

  Nutrition Expeditions—2nd and 4th grade curriculum packages on food groups and food choices.
  www.nutritionexploration.org

- U.S. Department of Agriculture—USDA.gov
  MyPlate.gov—Food and Nutrition Services

  MyPyramid.gov—information on the new food guide pyramid for adults and kids
  www.Teamnutrition.usda.gov—nutrition education resources for educators, parents, students, child care providers, etc.

## Getting Started with MyPlate

### MyPlate Icon

* MyPlate is part of a larger communications initiative based on *2010 Dietary Guidelines for Americans* to help consumers make better food choices.
* MyPlate is designed to *remind* Americans to eat healthfully; it is not intended to change consumer behavior alone.
* MyPlate illustrates the five food groups using a familiar mealtime visual, a place setting.

### ChooseMyPlate.gov

* The website features practical information and tips to help Americans build healthier diets.
* It features selected messages to help consumers focus on key behaviors. Selected messages include:
* **Balancing Calories**
  • Enjoy your food, but eat less.
  • Avoid oversized portions.
* **Foods to Increase**
  • Make half your plate fruits and vegetables.
  • Make at least half your grains whole grains.
  • Switch to fat-free or low-fat (1%) milk.
* **Foods to Reduce**
  • Compare sodium in foods like soup, bread, and frozen meals—and choose foods with lower numbers.
  • Drink water instead of sugary drinks.
* Choose**MyPlate**.gov includes much of the consumer and professional information formerly found on MyPyramid.gov.

## Consumer Resources: Let's Eat for the Health of It

### The 2010 Dietary Guidelines Brochure

This brochure contains practical strategies to make healthy food choices. The Brochure highlights themes from the Guidelines such as *Balancing Calories, Foods to Reduce,* and *Foods to Increase.* This resource is available online as a PDF.

### 10 Tips Nutrition Education Series

The 10 Tips Nutrition Education Series provides consumers and professionals with easy-to-follow tips in a convenient, printable format. Educators can use them to support existing lessons, and consumers can choose one or more of these tip sheets to start making small changes toward healthier eating. These and many other printable items are also available in Spanish.

### Also on the Web

* Sample Menus for a Week
* Food Group Based Recipes
* Historical Development of Food Guidance
* Nutrition Communicators Network for Partners – Application Forms
* All print-ready content

### MyPlate Style Guide

USDA encourages the use of the MyPlate icon in a variety of applications, including textbooks and other educational materials. Any educator or consumer interested in using the image should refer to this Guide for all appropriate information.

# Anatomy of MyPyramid

### One size doesn't fit all

USDA's new MyPyramid symbolizes a personalized approach to healthy eating and physical activity. The symbol has been designed to be simple. It has been developed to remind consumers to make healthy food choices and to be active every day. The different parts of the symbol are described below.

**Activity**
Activity is represented by the steps and the person climbing them, as a reminder of the importance of daily physical activity.

**Moderation**
Moderation is represented by the narrowing of each food group from bottom to top. The wider base stands for foods with little or no solid fats or added sugars. These should be selected more often. The narrower top area stands for foods containing more added sugars and solid fats. The more active you are, the more of these foods can fit into your diet.

**Personalization**
Personalization is shown by the person on the steps, the slogan, and the URL. Find the kinds and amounts of food to eat each day at MyPyramid.gov.

**Proportionality**
Proportionality is shown by the different widths of the food group bands. The widths suggest how much food a person should choose from each group. The widths are just a general guide, not exact proportions. Check the Web site for how much is right for you.

**Variety**
Variety is symbolized by the 6 color bands representing the 5 food groups of the Pyramid and oils. This illustrates that foods from all groups are needed each day for good health.

**Gradual Improvement**
Gradual improvement is encouraged by the slogan. It suggests that individuals can benefit from taking small steps to improve their diet and lifestyle each day.

USDA U.S. Department of Agriculture
Center for Nutrition Policy
and Promotion
April 2005 CNPP-16

USDA is an equal opportunity provider and employer.

| GRAINS | VEGETABLES | FRUITS | OILS | MILK | MEAT & BEANS |

ChooseMyPlate.gov

| GRAINS<br>Make half your grains whole | VEGETABLES<br>Vary your veggies | FRUITS<br>Focus on fruits | MILK<br>Get your calcium-rich foods | MEAT & BEANS<br>Go lean with protein |
|---|---|---|---|---|
| Eat at least 3 oz. of whole-grain cereals, breads, crackers, rice, or pasta every day<br><br>1 oz. is about 1 slice of bread, about 1 cup of breakfast cereal, or ½ cup of cooked rice, cereal, or pasta | Eat more dark-green veggies like broccoli, spinach, and other dark leafy greens<br><br>Eat more orange vegetables like carrots and sweetpotatoes<br><br>Eat more dry beans and peas like pinto beans, kidney beans, and lentils | Eat a variety of fruit<br><br>Choose fresh, frozen, canned, or dried fruit<br><br>Go easy on fruit juices | Go low-fat or fat-free when you choose milk, yogurt, and other milk products<br><br>If you don't or can't consume milk, choose lactose-free products or other calcium sources such as fortified foods and beverages | Choose low-fat or lean meats and poultry<br><br>Bake it, broil it, or grill it<br><br>Vary your protein routine — choose more fish, beans, peas, nuts, and seeds |

**For a 2,000-calorie diet, you need the amounts below from each food group. To find the amounts that are right for you, go to MyPyramid.gov.**

| Eat 6 oz. every day | Eat 2½ cups every day | Eat 2 cups every day | Get 3 cups every day; for kids aged 2 to 8, it's 2 | Eat 5½ oz. every day |
|---|---|---|---|---|

### Find your balance between food and physical activity

- Be sure to stay within your daily calorie needs.
- Be physically active for at least 30 minutes most days of the week.
- About 60 minutes a day of physical activity may be needed to prevent weight gain.
- For sustaining weight loss, at least 60 to 90 minutes a day of physical activity may be required.
- Children and teenagers should be physically active for 60 minutes every day, or most days.

### Know the limits on fats, sugars, and salt (sodium)

- Make most of your fat sources from fish, nuts, and vegetable oils.
- Limit solid fats like butter, margarine, shortening, and lard, as well as foods that contain these.
- Check the Nutrition Facts label to keep saturated fats, *trans* fats, and sodium low.
- Choose food and beverages low in added sugars. Added sugars contribute calories with few, if any, nutrients.

**MyPyramid.gov**
STEPS TO A HEALTHIER YOU

U.S. Department of Agriculture
Center for Nutrition Policy and Promotion
April 2005
CNPP-15

USDA is an equal opportunity provider and employer.

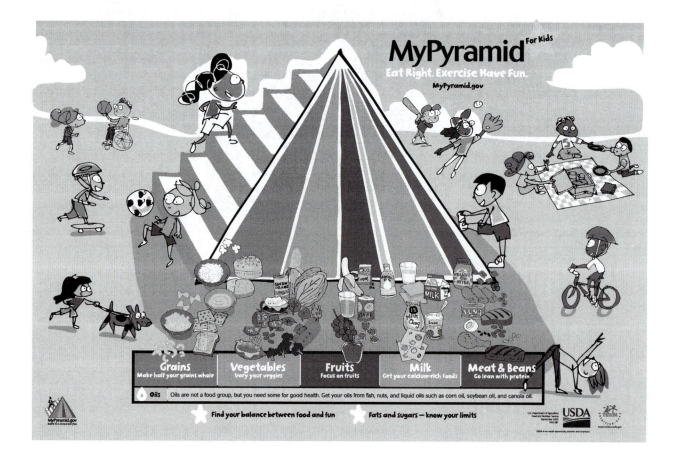

# What Do You Drink?

## It Makes More Difference Than You Think!

Calories in drinks are not hidden (they're listed right on the Nutrition Facts label), but many people don't realize just how many calories beverages can contribute to their daily intake. As you can see in the example on the next page, calories from drinks can really add up. But there is good news: you have plenty of options for reducing the number of calories in what you drink.

Substituting no—or low—calorie drinks for sugar-sweetened beverages cuts about 650 calories in the example on the previous page.

Of course, not everyone drinks the amount of sugar-sweetened beverages shown. Check the list below to estimate how many calories you typically take in from beverages.

| Type of Beverage | Calories in 12 oz | Calories in 20 oz |
| --- | --- | --- |
| Fruit punch | 192 | 320 |
| 100% apple juice | 180 | 300 |
| 100% orange juice | 168 | 280 |
| Lemonade | 168 | 280 |
| Regular lemon/lime soda | 148 | 247 |
| Regular cola | 136 | 227 |
| Sweetened lemon iced tea (bottled, not homemade) | 135 | 225 |
| Tonic water | 124 | 207 |
| Regular ginger ale | 124 | 207 |
| Sports drink | 99 | 165 |
| Fitness water | 18 | 36 |
| Unsweetened iced tea | 2 | 3 |
| Diet soda (with aspartame) | 0* | 0* |
| Carbonated water (unsweetened) | 0 | 0 |
| Water | 0 | 0 |

*Some diet soft drinks can contain a small number of calories that are not listed on the Nutrition Facts label. (USDA National Nutrient Database for Standard Reference)

## Learn To Read Nutrition Facts Carefully

Be aware that the Nutrition Facts label on beverage containers may give the calories for only part of the contents. The example below shows the label on a 20-oz. bottle. As you can see, it lists the number of calories in an 8-oz. serving (100) even though the bottle contains 20 oz. or 2.5 servings. To figure out how many calories are in the whole bottle, you need to multiply the number of calories in one serving by the number of servings in the bottle ($100 \times 2.5$). You can see that the contents of the entire bottle actually contain 250 calories even though what the label calls a "serving" only contains 100. This shows that you need to look closely at the serving size when comparing the calorie content of different beverages.

| NUTRITION FACTS LABEL | |
| --- | --- |
| Serving Size 8 fl, oz. | |
| Servings Per Container | 2.5 |
| **Amount per serving** | |
| Calories | 100 |

## High-Calorie Culprits in Unexpected Places

Coffee drinks and blended fruit smoothies sound innocent enough, but the calories in some of your favorite coffee-shop or smoothie stand items may surprise you. Check the website or in-store nutrition information of your favorite coffee or smoothie shop to find out how many calories are in different menu items.

# Dietary Supplements

Supplements are defined by law as any products intended to supplement the diet that contains a vitamin, a mineral, an herb, or other botanical; an amino acid; or a dietary substance for use by man to supplement the diet by increasing the total dietary intake.

Food and Drug Administration (FDA)—dietary substances include enzymes or tissues from animals organs or glands.

Dietary Supplement Health and Education Act (DSHEA) (1994)—clarified that supplements were to be regulated as foods, not drugs, and were therefore exempt from the tougher regulations accorded to drugs, such as requirements to prove that they are both safe and effective.

- no supplement has been demonstrated to be safe and effective under the rigorous FDA standards.
- drug companies do not have to report any unexpected or serious adverse events to the FDA (as they do with drugs).
- manufacturers of supplements may not make health claims when promoting a supplement but they may make structure or function claim—cannot say that their product "treats the symptoms of . . ." (a health claim) but can say "promotes health" (a structure or function claim).

**Most valid/reliable studies show that dietary supplements offer no benefits to well-nourished adults eating a Western diet and, in many cases, may be harmful.

# Eating Disorders

### Definitions:
- Eating disorders (EDs) are, most often, about more than food. Although they may start as a preoccupation with weight or body image, EDs are very complex and arise from a combination of long-standing behavioral, emotional, biological, psychological, social, and interpersonal factors. Control of food is used in an attempt to compensate for feelings and emotions that the person may otherwise find overwhelming to them. EDs can be symptoms of excessively compulsive behavior that manifests itself in control of food consumption.

- EDs do not discriminate and can affect anyone regardless of age, race, gender, sexual orientation, SES, or disability.

- Eating disorders can be the result of low self-esteem, troubled family or personal relationships, physical or sexual abuse, cultural norms or pressures, biological or genetic factors.

### Signs:
- Preoccupation with food and/or calories
- Significant weight loss
- Withdrawal from activities and friends
- Not eating or eating very little for an extended period of time
- Translucent skin, darkness under the eyes, bloating
- Wearing large or baggy clothes
- Being cold
- Checking weight excessively

### Types:
- *Anorexia:* self-induced starvation
- *Bulimia:* periods of overeating followed by purging through vomiting, use of diuretics and laxatives, fasting, or overexercising.
- *Binge Eating:* consumption of large amounts of food without compensation afterward. Labeling of foods "good" or "bad."
- *Anorexia Athletica:* also known as compulsive or obligatory exercise. Compelled by guilt or anxiety to continually work out.

### Help:
If you think that one of your students may have an eating disorder, follow appropriate reporting protocol. It can be a matter of life and death.

U.S. Dept. of Health and Human Services
National Institutes of Health
Womenshealth.gov
American College Health Association

_____

Department of Health & Human Services. Centers for Disease Control and Prevention.

# Fitness Testing

Used to determine current level of fitness in three areas
- Cardiovascular fitness
- Strength
- Flexibility
  - Can be used to help determine activities used during class while satisfying curriculum goals
  - Can be used as a pre/post test to determine the effects/success of a physical education program
  - Can be used to compare students to national norms

President's Council on Physical Fitness

Fitness Gram

Physical Best
- Healthy Fitness Zone
  - Norms by age and gender
  - No competition among students

Sample Test Items—Fitness Gram
- Pacer—cardiovascular
- Modified pull-ups—strength
- Modified sit-ups—strength
- Sit and reach—flexibility
- Trunk lift—flexibility

# Stretching Protocols: General Guidelines

## Static Stretching Activities

Recall, there are three common procedures of flexibility training. These include ballistic, static, and proprioceptive neuromuscular facilitation. Specific guidelines to each procedure have been described in Chapter 8. For reader ease, the recommended flexibility activities have been grouped according to specific flexibility training procedure.

It is important to emphasize that these activities are recommendations only. Individual differences in factors such as age, existing joint range of motion, disabilities, and muscular strength and endurance may influence the appropriateness of the activities. Activities that present greater risk of injury have been identified. These activities should be avoided (see Contraindicated Static Stretching Activities).

Individuals presenting recent soft tissue injuries to either the musculotendinous unit (strain) or ligaments (sprains) should avoid participation. Those presenting joint inflammation resulting from infections, known or suspected osteoporosis, unusual or unexplained tissue discomfort during elongation or other types of medical complications should limit flexibility training until they have established medical clearance.

To allow for maximal benefit and minimal risk of injury, several general guidelines should be followed. These guidelines may be fitted to any of the procedures or recommended flexibility activities.

As may be expected, first and foremost, is to establish medical clearance before beginning any flexibility training program. Any limitations and/or precautions should be clearly identified and understood by the participant and the exercise leader (if appropriate).

Warmup before any stretching activities. Warm-up activities, such as light calisthenics and walking/jogging are appropriate. The critical issue is to raise core body temperature. The exact time and nature of required warm-up activities may vary. When possible, identify the muscle groups you intend to include in flexibility training. Be sure these muscle groups are adequately warmed up **before** stretching activities are performed.

Wear clothes that are non-restrictive. All joint structures should be able to move through a full range of motion. Avoid footwear and exercise mats that allow skidding. Unwanted slipping of body parts such as feet or hands may result in injury.

Perform all stretching routines in a controlled, slow, and non-jerky manner. Never bounce or force a muscle through a range of motion. Focus your mind on the muscles involved. Try to relax the active tissue. Avoid rapid movements that may induce the stretch-reflex mechanism. Return from stretched positions slowly and carefully. Always determine the appropriate postural position to be used before beginning any stretching activity. Table 3.1 summarizes the sequence of action for static stretching activities.

Avoid breath holding. Normal, free breathing patterns should be included in flexibility training. It may be beneficial to control breathing. Many find it beneficial and relaxing to sequence a deep exhalation with the more extreme ranges of motion.

From *Concepts of Health-Related Fitness* by Thomas M. Adams, II. Copyright © 2002 by Thomas M. Adams, II. Reprinted by permission.

**Table 3.1** Sequence of action for static stretching activities

| Step | Action |
|------|--------|
| 1 | Assume the recommended body position and slowly stretch the selected muscle tissue to a point of end range of motion. |
| 2 | Slowly apply mild tension to passively stretch the selected muscle tissue to a point of mild discomfort. Slowly exhale during the stretch. |
| 3 | Hold the passive stretched position for 10–30 seconds. |
| 4 | Relax the tissue by slowly returning the selected muscle tissue to normal resting length. |
| 5 | Repeat steps 1–4 a minimum of 4 times per stretching activity. |

Finally, remember to use caution when relaxing a muscle from a stretched position. Always return a muscle slowly and carefully to its natural resting length. As in the case when stretching a muscle, avoid rapid and jerky movements.

## Contraindicated Static Stretching Activities

Individual differences in variables such as age, soft tissue characteristics, muscular strength and endurance, disabilities and fitness levels may predetermine the appropriateness of some flexibility training activities. The exercises described below should be considered **inappropriate for general use**. Simply stated, they offer too much risk of injury for the general public.

That is not to say that some, if not all, of these flexibility training activities are not used by highly trained and fit individuals. This of course leads to much of the confusion surrounding these activities.

Individuals who regularly train or participate in activities such as dance, gymnastics, martial arts, wrestling, and yoga may find these higher risk training procedures present less risk of injury. This, of course, is a direct result of the advanced levels of flexibility training required for these activities. It must be emphasized; this finding is true for only those participants who have an established, advanced levels of flexibility. Participants new to these types of activities should use caution and train using the flexibility activities recommended for the general public.

**Figure 3.7**     Plough

### Plough
**Potential Risk:** The plough flexibility training procedure places unwanted and unnecessarily high levels of strain on the cervical ligaments of the lower back (see Figure 3.7). Additionally, increased and potentially excessive pressure is placed on the cervical discs. The plough procedure should be considered extremely dangerous for individuals presenting a history of low back complications.

### Hurdler's Stretch
**Potential Risk:** The single or double legged hurdler's stretch (see Figure 3.8) places unwanted and unnecessarily high levels of strain on the medial collateral ligament of the knee. Additionally, increased and potentially excessive pressure is placed on the meniscus of the knee. This pressure leads to increased risk of meniscal tears. The hurdler's stretch should be considered extremely

**Figure 3.8**     Hurdlers Stretch

Kendall Hunt

**Figure 3.9**     Full or Deep Knee Squats or Lunges

**Figure 3.10**     Standing Straight Legged Toe Touch

Kendall Hunt

dangerous for individuals presenting a history of knee joint complications. This is particularly true for those with a history of ligamental and/or menisci trauma or tears.

### Full or Deep Knee Squats or Lunges

**Potential Risk:** Full or deep knee squats or lunges are defined as squatting or lunging movements that allow for knee flexion of 90 degree or greater (see Figure 3.9). A practical, easily observable criteria to prevent excessive knee flexion would be to limit movements that allow for the knee to be moved or positioned over the ankle. Full or deep knee squats or lunges place unwanted and unnecessarily high levels of strain on the lateral ligaments of the knee. Additionally, increased and potentially excessive patellar tendon forces, occurring during knee flexion, compress the patella (kneecap). This pressure leads to increased risk of chrondomalacia and/or meniscal tears. Full or deep knee squats or lunges should be considered extremely dangerous for individuals presenting a history of knee joint complications. This is particularly true for those with a history of ligamental and/or menisci trauma or tears.

### Standing Straight Legged Toe Touch

**Potential Risk:** The standing straight legged toe touch flexibility procedure places unwanted and unnecessarily high levels of strain on the lumbar ligaments (see Figure 3.10). Additionally, increased and potentially excessive pressure is placed on the lumbar (lower vertebrae of the back) discs. The standing straight legged toe touch procedure should be considered extremely dangerous for individuals presenting a history of low back complications.

### Standing Straight Legged Straddle Toe Touch

**Potential Risk:** Similar to the standing straight legged toe touch, the standing straight legged straddle toe touch flexibility procedure places unwanted and unnecessarily high levels of strain on the lumbar ligaments (see Figure 3.11). Additionally, increased and potentially excessive pressure is placed on the lumbar (lower vertebrae of the back) discs. If flexion occurs with rotation, such as in the case of moving the head toward one leg, shear or torsion forces are also placed on spinal disc. Lastly, the straddle position places unnecessarily high levels of strain on the medial collateral ligaments of the knees. The standing straight legged straddle toe touch procedure should be considered extremely dangerous for individuals presenting a history of low back and knee joint complications.

### Full Neck Rolls

**Potential Risks:** Full neck rolls place unwanted and unnecessarily high levels of strain on the cervical ligaments (see Figure 3.12). Additionally, increased and potentially excessive pressure is placed on the cervical discs. Lastly, a potential for arterial impingement may occur resulting in restricted blood flow and dizziness or syncope (temporary loss of consciousness).

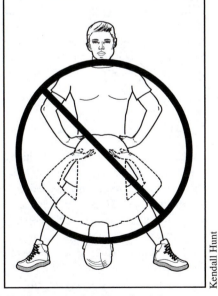

Kendall Hunt

**Figure 3.11**     Standing Straight Legged Toe Touch

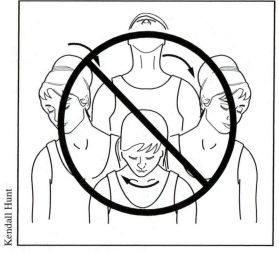

**Figure 3.12**    Full Neck Rolls

**Figure 3.13**    Waist Circles

### Waist Circles

**Potential Risks:** Waist circles place unwanted and unnecessarily high levels of strain on the lower back musculature (see Figure 3.13). Additionally, increased and potentially excessive pressure is placed on the lumbar vertebrae of the lower back.

### Back Bends (Bridges)

**Potential Risks:** Back bends (Bridges) hyperextend the lower back (see Figure 3.14). This action places unwanted and unnecessarily high levels of stress on the vertebral disc located in the lumbar region of the spine.

## Recommended Static Stretching Activities

Many appropriate static stretching activities could be recommended. If properly incorporated into a regular flexibility training program, each would allow for positive gains in joint range of motion. To illustrate and describe such a large number of procedures is beyond the scope of this manuscript. As a result, a sampling of the more common procedures has been provided. For reader ease, procedures have been grouped by body segment.

### Feet

#### Plantar Arch

**Procedure:** Assume a standing position facing a wall. Stand approximately two feet away from the wall. Place your hands on the wall, at approximately chest level, in front of you for balance. While bending one leg, extend the other leg straight backward keeping the foot flat and pointed directly toward the wall. To stretch the plantar arch, raise the heel of the extended foot, bending the toes at the ball of the foot. Carefully shift more of your body weight onto the ball of this foot while pressing downward on the toes (see Figure 3.15). You should be able to control the tension of the stretch by how you shift your weight. Hold the stretch for approximately 10–30 seconds and then relax by shifting your weight off the extended leg to the nondominant foot. Repeat a minimum of four repetitions. Switch foot positions and repeat the procedure.

**Figure 3.14**    Back Bends (Bridges)

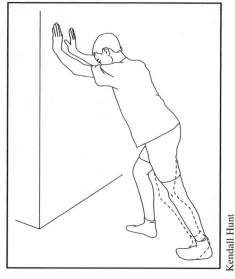

**Figure 3.15**    Plantar Arch Stretch

### Anterior Foot and Toes

**Procedure:** Assume a standing position with your body weight resting on a support leg. Position the other leg so the anterior foot and toes of the foot are plantar flexed or pointed and resting on the ground. Turn the toes of the foot under so the pressure can be felt on the top of the curled toes on the active leg. To stretch the anterior foot and toes, carefully shift your body weight onto the active leg, pressing downward on the top of the toes until tension is felt (see Figure 3.16). Hold the stretch for approximately 10–30 seconds and then relax by shifting your weight back to the support leg. Repeat a minimum of four repetitions. Switch foot positions and repeat the procedure.

### Lower Legs

### Anterior Lower Leg

**Procedure #1:** One of the more common methods of stretching the anterior aspect of the lower leg is to simply assume a kneeling position and then sit back on your heels while your feet are plantar flexed (see Figure 3.17). The feet may be placed directly on the floor or on a flat cushion or other soft surface. Shifting body weight on or off the heels controls the tension of the stretch. Hold the stretch for approximately 10–30 seconds and then relax by leaning forward and shifting body weight onto the knees. Repeat a minimum of four repetitions. **This activity should be considered contraindicated and avoided for individuals presenting knee limitations.**

**Procedure #2**: An alternative method of stretching the anterior aspect of the lower leg for individuals with knee limitations is to assume a sitting position in a chair or bench of normal height. Cross one leg and rest the ankle of this leg on the knee of the support leg. Plantar flex the foot of this leg. Grasp the toes of the foot on the crossed leg with one hand and the ankle with the other. Slowly pull the toes of the foot toward your body while stabilizing the leg at the ankle with the other hand (see Figure 3.18). Control the tension of the stretch by how hard you pull on the foot. Hold the stretch for approximately 10–30 seconds and then relax by releasing the pull. Repeat the procedure a minimum of four repetitions. Switch leg, foot, and hand positions and repeat the procedure.

**Figure 3.16**   Anterior Foot and Toes Stretch

**Figure 3.17**   Anterior Lower Leg Stretch
Procedure #1

### Lateral Lower Leg

**Procedure:** To stretch the lateral (outside) aspect of the lower leg, assume a sitting position in a chair or bench of normal height. Cross one leg and rest the ankle of this leg on the knee of the support leg. Grasp the toes and outside portion of the foot on the crossed leg with one hand and the ankle with the other. Slowly invert the foot toward your body while stabilizing the leg at the ankle with the other hand (see Figure 3.19). Control the tension of the stretch by how hard you pull and lift the foot during inversion. Hold the stretch for approximately 10–30 seconds and then relax by releasing the pull. Repeat the procedure a minimum of four repetitions. Switch leg, foot, and hand positions and repeat the procedure.

### Posterior Lower Leg

**Procedure:** Assume a standing position facing a wall. Stand several feet away from the wall. Place your hands on the wall, at approximately chest level, in front of you for balance. While bending one leg, fully extend the other leg straight backward keeping the foot flat and pointed directly toward the wall until your body is linearly extended from head to foot. To stretch the posterior lower leg, carefully shift your body weight forward while keeping the

**Figure 3.18** Anterior Lower Leg Stretch
Procedure #2

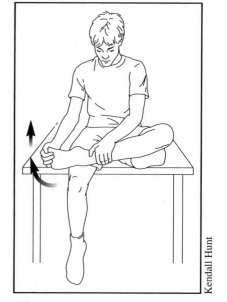

**Figure 3.19** Lateral Lower Leg
Stretch

foot of the extended leg flat on the floor (see Figure 3.20). You should be able to control the tension of the stretch by how you shift your weight. Hold the stretch for approximately 10–30 seconds and then relax by shifting your weight off the extended leg to the nondominant foot. Repeat a minimum of four repetitions. Switch foot positions and repeat the procedure. Individuals presenting physical limitations with their knees should avoid locking out the knee on the extended leg.

## Upper Legs

### Anterior Upper Leg

**Procedure:** Assume a standing position facing a wall. Stand approximately two feet from the wall. Extend one arm, at approximately chest level, in front of you for balance. Shift your body weight to the nonactive leg or the leg opposite of the extended arm. Bend your knee and raise the heel of the active leg toward your buttocks. Reach behind your hip with the same side arm as the active leg and grasp the raised foot of the active leg. To stretch the anterior upper leg muscles, collectively

**Figure 3.20** Posterior Lower Leg Stretch

referred to as the quadriceps, lift or pull up on the heel bringing it toward your buttocks (see Figure 3.21). **Individuals presenting physical limitations with their knees should avoid fixing the active leg against the support leg during stretching.** To help eliminate risk of injury to the active knee, allow the knee of the active leg to drift backwards, hyperextending the active upper leg at the hip. Control the tension of the stretch by controlling the magnitude of the lifting force. Hold each stretch for approximately 10–30 seconds and then relax by releasing and lowering the heel of the active foot. Repeat a minimum of four repetitions. Switch foot and hand positions and repeat the procedure.

### Posterior Upper Leg

**Procedure:** Assume a standing position facing a bench or chair of standard height. Shift your body weight to your support leg and raise the active leg and rest the heel of the foot of this leg on the surface of the chair or bench. To stretch the posterior upper leg muscles, collectively referred to as the hamstrings, keep both legs straight and bend forward at the waist, lowering your head and upper body to the raised leg. Precaution should be taken to keep your back straight (see Figure 3.22). Control the tension of the stretch by how far you lower your upper body or how closely you bring your upper body

**Figure 3.21**     Anterior Upper Leg Stretch

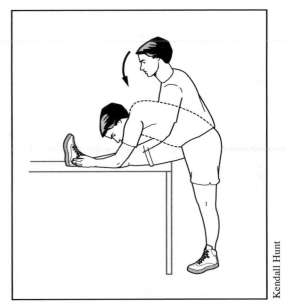

**Figure 3.22**     Posterior Upper Leg Stretch

to the extended leg. **Individuals presenting physical limitations with their knees should avoid locking out the knees**. Hold each stretch for approximately 10–30 seconds and then relax by lifting your upper body and standing back up. Repeat a minimum of four repetitions. Switch foot and leg positions and repeat the procedure.

### Adductors

**Procedure:** Assume a sitting position on the floor. Bring the soles of both feet together by flexing both knees and pulling the heels of the feet toward your crotch and buttocks. Keeping your back fully extended, place your elbows and lower arms on the same side knee. To stretch the adductors, use your elbows and lower arms to press your knees to the floor (see Figure 3.23). Control the tension of the stretch by how much pressure you place on the knees and how much you lower the knees toward the floor. Hold each stretch for approximately 10–30 seconds and then relax by releasing pressure and raising your knees. Repeat a minimum of four repetitions.

### Hips

**Procedure:** Assume a supine position on your back with both legs fully extended. To stretch the hip, flex one leg at the hip until the knee is directly over the hip. Grasp the flexed leg at the knee and ankle and slowly externally rotate the knee outward while simultaneously pulling the ankle to the opposite shoulder until the lower leg is held at approximately 90-degrees. Keep the head and shoulders flat on the floor at all times (see Figure 3.24). Hold each stretch for approximately 10–30 seconds and then relax by releasing the pull and lowering the leg back to its original position. Repeat a minimum of four repetitions for each leg, alternating legs.

### Back and Trunk

The following procedures describe those recommended in Chapter 12—Low Back Pain.

**Figure 3.23**     Adductor Stretch

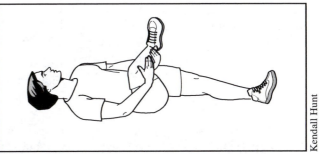

**Figure 3.24**     Hip Stretch

### Supine Single Leg Trunk Rotation

Assume a supine position on your back with both legs fully extended and each arm abducted out to the side, to a 90-degree angle from the long axis of the body. To stretch the lower back, keep one leg fully extended and cross the other leg over it at the hip level bringing the ankle and foot of the crossed leg to the extended hand. The hip of the crossed leg will rotate off the floor (see Figure 3.25). Control the tension of the stretch by how far you lower the crossed leg to the floor. The head, shoulders, and the fully extended leg should remain flat on the floor during the stretch. Hold each stretch for approximately 10–30 seconds and then relax by lowering the crossed leg and rotating the hips until both gluteal masses are back in contact with the floor. Repeat a minimum of four repetitions and then switch legs.

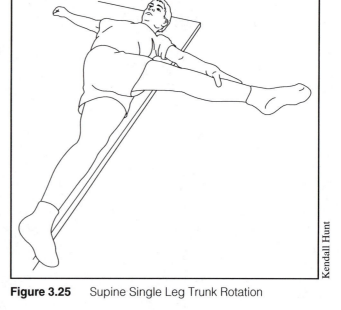

**Figure 3.25**    Supine Single Leg Trunk Rotation

### Supine Double Leg Hip Rotation

Assume a supine position on your back with your knees bent to approximately a 90-degree angle. Each arm should be abducted out to the side approximately 90 degrees from the long axis of the body. To stretch the lower back, slowly rotate both legs to the floor on one side of the body keeping the head, shoulders, and arms flat on the floor (see Figure 3.26). Control the tension of the stretch by controlling how far you lower your knees to the floor. Hold each stretch for approximately 10–30 seconds and then relax by rotating both legs back up to their original position. Repeat a minimum of four repetitions to each side, alternating sides.

**Figure 3.26**    Supine Double Leg Hip Rotation

### Cat Stretch

Assume a kneeling position. Position your hips directly over your knees and place your hands directly under your shoulders. Fully extend both arms. To stretch your lower back, slowly lower your head between your extended arms and fully round your lower back by contracting your abdominal musculature (see Figure 3.27). Control the tension of the stretch by how much you round your lower back. Hold each stretch for approximately 10–30 seconds and then relax by lifting your head and flattening your back. Repeat a minimum of four repetitions.

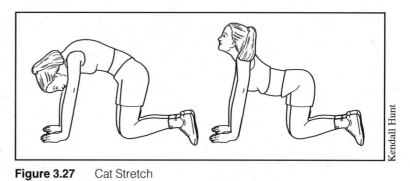

**Figure 3.27**    Cat Stretch

### Double Leg Hip Flexion

Assume a supine position on your back with both knees bent to approximately a 90-degree angle. To stretch your lower back, grasp behind each knee and pull both knees simultaneously toward your chest, rotating the hips off the floor (see Figure 3.28). Control the tension of the stretch by how far you pull the knees toward your chest. You may elect to keep your head and shoulders flat on the floor at all times. Hold each stretch for approximately 10–30 seconds and then relax by lowering your legs and rotating the hips back to their original position. Repeat a minimum of four times.

### Single Leg Hip Flexion

Assume a supine position on your back with both knees bent to approximately a 90-degree angle. To stretch your lower back, grasp one knee with both hands and slowly pull it toward your chest. Keep your head and shoulders flat on the floor at all times (see Figure 3.29). Control the tension of the stretch by how far you pull the knee toward the chest. Hold each stretch for approximately 10–30 seconds and then relax by lowering the leg to its original position. Repeat a minimum of four times for each leg, alternating legs.

**Figure 3.28**  Double Leg Hip Flexion

### Neck

#### Anterior

**Procedure:** Assume a standing or an upright sitting position. To stretch the anterior aspect of the neck, place both hands on the top, front of the head (forehead) and slowly press backward (see Figure 3.30). Control the tension of the stretch by how hard and far you push the head backward. **Precaution should be taken to avoid excessive pressure or force**. Hold each stretch for approximately 10–30 seconds and then relax by raising your head to an upright position. Repeat a minimum of four times.

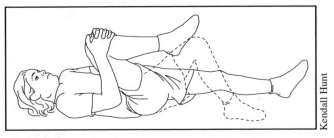

**Figure 3.29**  Single Leg Hip Flexion

#### Lateral

**Procedure:** Assume a standing or an upright sitting position. To stretch the lateral aspect of the neck reach over your head and grasp the opposite side of your head with your hand (see Figure 3.31). Slowly pull your head towards the shoulder of the reaching hand. Control the tension of the stretch by how hard and far you pull the head towards the shoulder. **Precaution should be taken to avoid excessive pressure or force**. Hold each stretch for approximately 10–30 seconds and then relax by raising your head to an upright position. Repeat a minimum of four times.

#### Posterior

**Procedure:** Assume a standing or an upright sitting position. To stretch the posterior neck grasp the top, back aspect of your head with both hands and slowly pull your head down so that your chin rests against your chest (see Figure 3.32). Control the tension of the stretch by how hard and far downward you pull your head. **Precaution should be taken to**

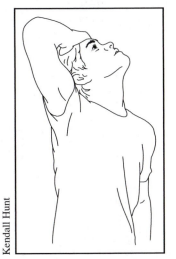

**Figure 3.30**  Anterior Neck Stretch

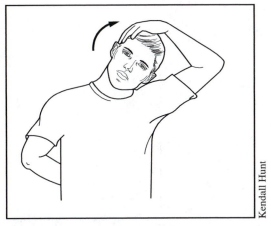

**Figure 3.31**  Lateral Neck Stretch

**Figure 3.32**    Posterior Neck Stretch

**Figure 3.33**    Chest Stretch

**avoid excessive pressure or force**. Hold each stretch for approximately 10–30 seconds and then relax by raising your head to an upright position. Repeat a minimum of four times.

## Chest

**Procedure:** Assume a standing position, facing perpendicular next to a wall. Raise one arm to chest level and place or affix your palm flat on the wall. To stretch the chest, rotate your body on its long axis away from the wall. To maximize the tension on the chest muscles, maintain a linear line from the midline of the body to the hand (see Figure 3.33). Control the tension of the stretch by how far you rotate your body. Hold each stretch for approximately 10–30 seconds and then relax by rotating your body back to its original position. Repeat a minimum of four times, alternating body positions and arms.

## Shoulders

### Anterior

**Procedure:** Assume a sitting position with your hands placed at shoulder width behind your hips. To stretch the anterior aspect of the shoulder, keeping your hands flat and pointed backwards, slide the hips forward (see Figure 3.34). Control the tension of the stretch by how far you slide your hips forward. Hold each stretch for approximately 10–30 seconds and then relax by shifting your hips back, decreasing the distance between your hips and hands. Repeat a minimum of four times.

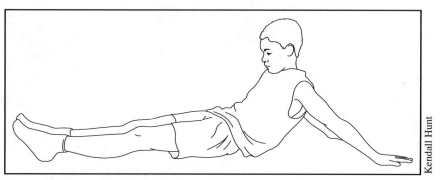

**Figure 3.34**    Anterior Shoulder Stretch

### Posterior

**Procedure:** Assume a standing or an upright sitting position. To stretch the posterior aspect of the shoulder, raise one arm to shoulder level and reach across your chest (see Figure 3.35). Using your other hand, grasp the elbow of the crossed arm and pull the elbow toward your chest. Control the tension of the stretch by how hard you pull the crossed arm toward your chest. Hold each stretch for approximately 10–30 seconds and then relax by lowering and returning the crossed arm to its original position. Repeat a minimum of four times, alternating arms.

### Arms

#### Anterior (Biceps)

**Procedure:** Assume a standing position, facing perpendicular next to a wall. Raise one arm to chest level and place or affix your palm flat on the wall. To stretch the biceps, rotate your body on its long axis away from the wall. To maximize the tension on the biceps, allow transverse hyperextension to occur at the shoulder (see Figure 3.36). Control the tension of the stretch by how far you rotate your body. Hold each stretch for approximately 10–30 seconds and then relax by rotating your body back to its original position. Repeat a minimum of four times, alternating body positions.

#### Posterior (Triceps)

**Procedure:** Assume a standing or an upright sitting position. Both arms should be relaxed and hanging naturally at the sides. Reach behind your head with one hand as if to scratch the middle of your back. To stretch the triceps, grasp the elbow of the reaching arm and hand, with the opposite hand, and press the elbow behind the head (see Figure 3.37). Control the tension of the stretch by how hard you press the elbow behind the head. Hold each stretch for approximately 10–30 seconds and then relax by lowering both arms to their original position. Repeat a minimum of four times, alternating arms.

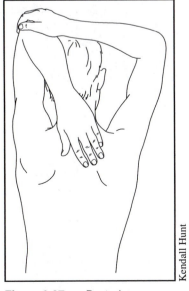

**Figure 3.35**   Posterior Shoulder Stretch

**Figure 3.36**   Anterior Upper Arm (Biceps) Stretch

**Figure 3.37**   Posterior Upper Arm (Triceps) Stretch

## Ballistic Stretching Activities

Because of the inherent danger associated with ballistic stretching, no ballistic stretching activities are recommended.

## Proprioceptive Neuromuscular Facilitation Stretching Activities

There are many appropriate proprioceptive neuromuscular facilitation stretching activities that could be recommended. If properly incorporated into a regular flexibility training program each would allow for positive gains in joint range of motion. To illustrate and describe such a large number of procedures is beyond the scope of this manuscript. As a result, a sampling of the more common procedures has been provided. For reader ease, procedures have been grouped by body segment. To control page space, fewer activities, as compared to static stretches, are offered. Table 3.2 offers an overall step sequence used in all PNF activities. Step 1 is illustrated in Figure 3.38. Steps 2 & 3 are illustrated in Figure 3.39. Steps 4–6 are illustrated in Figure 3.40.

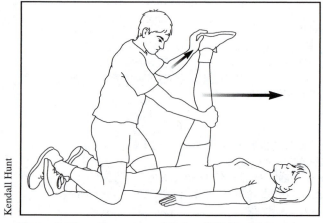

**Figure 3.38**  Sequence of Action PNF Stretching Step 1

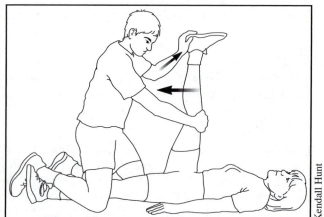

**Figure 3.39**  Sequence of Action PNF Stretching Steps 2 and 3

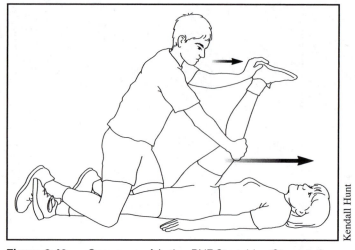

**Figure 3.40**  Sequence of Action PNF Stretching Steps 4–6

**Table 3.2** Sequence of action for proprioceptive neuromuscular facilitation stretching activities

| Step | Action |
|------|--------|
| 1 | Assume the recommended body position and slowly stretch the selected muscle tissue to a point of end range of motion. |
| 2 | Have a partner or use an external apparatus to stabilize the body segment at the point of end range of motion. |
| 3 | Submaximally isometrically contract the selected muscle tissue for 6 seconds while the body segment is being stabilized. |
| 4 | Following the isometric contraction, have a partner slowly apply mild force in a direction to passively stretch the selected muscle tissue. |
| 5 | Hold the passive stretched for 10–30 seconds. |
| 6 (Optional) | Subject may contract agonist muscle group at the same time the partner is passively stretching the selected muscle tissue. |
| 7 | Relax the tissue by slowly returning the selected muscle tissue to normal resting length. |
| 8 | Repeat steps 1–7 a minimum of 4 times per stretching activity. |

## Upper Leg

### Anterior

**Procedure**: Assume a supine position on your stomach. To stretch the anterior leg (quadriceps) and hip flexors, raise one leg while keeping your chest, arms, head, and opposite leg in contact with the floor. Stretch the quadriceps and hip flexors to a point of mild discomfort. Have a partner stabilize the raised leg in this position (see Figure 3.41). Then, isometrically contract the quadriceps and hip flexors for approximately six seconds. **Precaution should be taken to avoid maximal isometric contraction particularly at end range of motion**. Following contraction, actively elongate the quadriceps and hip flexors by contracting the hamstrings and gluteal musculature, or have your partner passively stretch the quadriceps and hip flexors by carefully and slowly lifting up on the knee. Hold this position for approximately 10–30 seconds. To relax, slowly lower the leg to the floor. Repeat this procedure a minimum of four times for each leg, alternating legs.

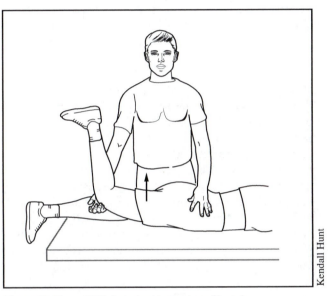

**Figure 3.41**    PNF Anterior Upper Leg Stretch

### Posterior

**Procedure**: Assume a supine position on your back on the floor. To stretch the posterior upper leg (hamstrings), raise one leg while keeping your head, hips, and back in contact with the floor, stretching the hamstrings to a point of mild discomfort. Have your partner stabilize the leg in this position (see Figure 3.42). Then, isometrically contract the hamstring musculature for approximately six seconds. **Precaution should be taken to avoid maximal isometric contraction particularly at end range of motion.** Following contraction, actively elongate the hamstrings by contracting the iliopsoas musculature (hip flexors), or have your partner passively stretch the hamstrings by carefully and slowly pushing your heel toward your head. Hold this position for approximately 10–30 seconds. To relax, slowly lower the leg to the floor. Repeat this procedure a minimum of four times for each leg, alternating legs.

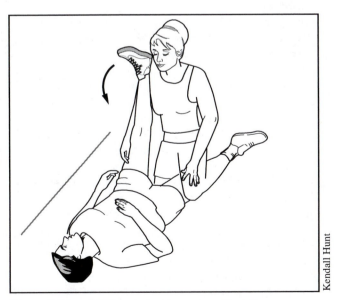

**Figure 3.42**    PNF Posterior Upper Leg Stretch

### Lower Back

**Procedure**: Assume a sitting position on the floor with your legs fully extended in front of you. Do not lock the knees out. To stretch the lower back, gradually lean forward, as if attempting to touch your toes, stretching the musculature of the lower back to a point of mild discomfort. Have your partner stabilize the back in this position (see Figure 3.43). Then, isometrically contract the low back musculature for approximately six seconds. **Precaution should be taken to avoid maximal isometric contraction particularly at end range of motion**. Following contraction, actively elongate the low back musculature by contracting the abdominal musculature, or have your partner passively stretch the low back by pressing on your shoulders for approximately 10–30 seconds. To relax, slowly sit back up. Repeat this procedure a minimum of four times.

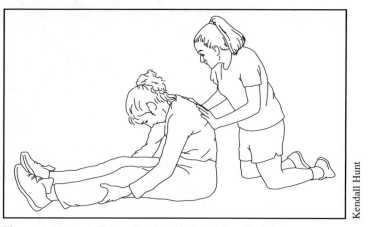

**Figure 3.43**    PNF Low Back and Hamstring Stretch

### Chest

**Procedure**: Assume a sitting position on the floor with your hands placed behind your head. To stretch the chest draw your elbows back behind your head until you stretch the musculature of the chest to a point of mild discomfort. Have your partner stabilize your arms, by grasping your elbows, in this position (see Figure 3.44). Then, isometrically contract the chest musculature for approximately six seconds. **Precaution should be taken to avoid maximal isometric contraction particularly at end range of motion**. Following contraction, actively elongate the chest musculature by contracting the rhomboids, posterior deltoids and back (trapezius) musculature, or have your partner passively stretch the chest by pulling on your arms for approximately 10–30 seconds. To relax, slowly allow the elbows to move forward. Repeat this procedure a minimum of four times.

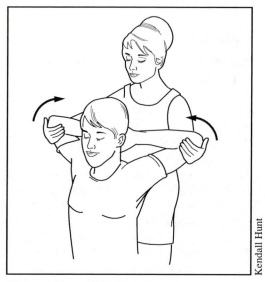

**Figure 3.44**    PNF Chest Stretch

### Shoulders

**Procedure**: Assume a standing position facing away from your partner. To stretch the shoulder musculature, hyperextend your arms behind you until you stretch the shoulders to a point of mild discomfort. Have your partner stabilize your arms in this position by grasping your wrists and lifting up (see Figure 3.45). Then, isometrically contract your shoulders while attempting to lower your stabilized arms for approximately six seconds. **Precaution should be taken to avoid maximal isometric contraction particularly at end range of motion**. Following contraction, actively elongate the shoulder musculature by attempting to further raise your arms behind you or by having your partner passively stretch the shoulders by lifting up on your arms for approximately 10–30 seconds. To relax, slowly lower your arms to your sides. Repeat this procedure a minimum of four times.

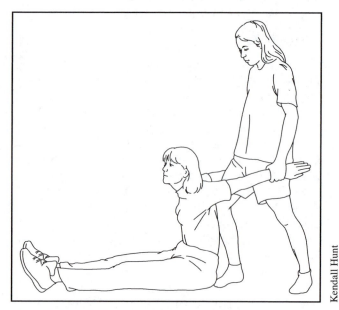

**Figure 3.45**    PNF Anterior Shoulder Stretch

## Adductors

**Procedure**: Assume a sitting position on the floor. Bring the soles of both feet together by flexing both knees and pulling the heels of the feet toward your crotch and buttocks. Keeping your back fully extended, relax your elbows and lower arms on your flexed legs. To stretch the adductors, lower your knees until you stretch the adductors to a point of mild discomfort. Have your partner stabilize your legs, by pressing down on the knees, in this position (see Figure 3.46). Then, isometrically contract the adductors for approximately six seconds. **Precaution should be taken to avoid maximal isometric contraction particularly at end range of motion**. Following contraction, actively elongate the adductors by contracting the leg abductors, or have your partner passively stretch the adductors by pressing down on your knees for approximately 10–30 seconds. To relax, slowly raise your knees. Repeat this procedure a minimum of four times.

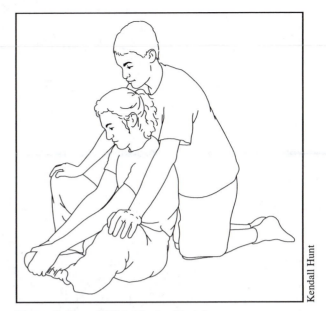

**Figure 3.46**    PNF Adductor Stretch

Kendall Hunt

# Appendix 1

*Assessment Forms*

## Lesson Plan Evaluation

Name _____
Activity/Developmental Level _____

1.  Objectives written correctly and match purpose      3    2.5    2    1.5    1    .5    0

2.  Activities match developmental level and curriculum focus      3    2.5    2    1.5    1    .5    0

3.  Logical sequence to instruction      3    2.5    2    1.5    1    .5    0

4.  Thoroughness of content      3    2.5    2    1.5    1    .5    0

5.  Considerations for facility/equipment/visual aids      3    2.5    2    1.5    1    .5    0

# Health Lesson Plan Evaluation

07E:127

Name _____

Activity/Developmental Level _____

| | 3 | 2.5 | 2 | 1.5 | 1 | .5 | 0 |
|---|---|---|---|---|---|---|---|
| 1. Objectives written correctly and match purpose | 3 | 2.5 | 2 | 1.5 | 1 | .5 | 0 |
| 2. Activities match developmental level and curriculum focus | 3 | 2.5 | 2 | 1.5 | 1 | .5 | 0 |
| 3. Logical sequence to instruction | 3 | 2.5 | 2 | 1.5 | 1 | .5 | 0 |
| 4. Thoroughness of content | 3 | 2.5 | 2 | 1.5 | 1 | .5 | 0 |
| 5. Considerations for facility/equipment/visual aids | 3 | 2.5 | 2 | 1.5 | 1 | .5 | 0 |

*Physical Education*

*Class Observation*

07E:127

**Name** _____
**School** _____
**Teacher** _____
**Date of Observation** _____

***When you arrive at the school, 1st go to the office and sign in as a visitor. Next, find the gym and <u>ask</u> the teacher if you may observe. 3rd, thank the teacher for their time, then report back to the main office and sign out. Turn this in no later than the last Monday of class.

1. What was the Developmental Level of the class which you observed?

2. In what activities were the students participating?

3. Developmentally, what was the purpose or curriculum focus of the lesson, ie: hand-eye coordination, sport skills, body management, etc?

4. Give a <u>brief</u> summary of the lesson and <u>your comments</u>.

# Appendix 2

*Resource Guide*

# Web Resources

## Government

### World Health Organization (WHO)
http://www.who.int/en/
This organization is the health authority within the United Nations system. Health topics, publications, and data and statistics can all be found on this site.

### United Stated Department of Health and Human Resources
http://www.hhs.gov/
This is the main governmental agency for protecting the health of Americans, while also providing human services. Information can be found on this site about numerous topics related to the health field.

### National Association of State Boards of Education (NASBE)
http://www.nasbe.org/
This nonprofit organization helps create safe and healthy environments in schools around the world. Some of their projects include healthy eating, HIV prevention, obesity prevention, and safe and healthy schools.

### National Institute of Health
http://www.nih.gov/
The National Institutes of Health are part of the U.S. Department of Health and Human Services. It is the primary agency for conducting and supporting medical research. On this website you can find an A-Z listing of consumer health topics, along with information on current events in the health field.

### National Institute on Drug Abuse
http://www.nida.nih.gov/
Part of the National Institutes of Health, this site offers education resources and materials for students, parents, teachers, medical and health professionals, and also researchers. There is information on programs offered, research, clinical trials, and upcoming meeting and events.

### Iowa Association for Health, Physical Education, Recreation and Dance (IAHPERD)
http://www.iowaahperd.org/index.html
IAHPERD uses national conventions, newsletters, journals and other resources to advocate for children to be healthy and active.

## Health

### American Association for Health Education (AAHE)
http://www.aahperd.org/aahe/
This association uses education and promotion strategies to assist health professionals and educators promote health. They provide professional development, programs and events, publication and networking, among other things, to further the cause of health for all people.

### American Dietetic Association (ADA)
http://www.eatright.org/
The ADA is a great source of science-based food and nutrition information. As the largest organization of food and nutrition professionals, the ADA offers information for the public, students, and health professionals.

### American Heart Association (AHA)
http://www.americanheart.org/presenter.ihtml?identifier=1200000
The AHA site contains information on taking care of your health and your heart. It has sections aimed at children's health, diseases, healthy lifestyle, among many more.

### Kids Health (Nemours Foundation)
http://kidshealth.org
The site provides health information separated into three categories: parents, teens, and kids. The parents area also provides health lessons for teachers. This health information is doctor approved, and includes age appropriate information including games.

### Learn to be Healthy
http://learntobehealthy.org
An online health science education center designed to help parents, teachers, and students learn about health and health related topics. Provides lesson plans, educational games and activites and interactive webquest.

**Muscular Dystrophy Association (MDA)**

www.mda.org

The MDA site contains a huge amount of information about muscular dystrophy, and other neuromuscular diseases. There is information on research and clinical trials, support groups, clinics, and much more.

**Food and Nutrition Service (FNS)**

www.fns.usda.gov

The FNS administers the nutrition assistance programs of the U.S. Department of Agriculture. Their mission is a healthier diet and better access to food to children and families in need. It is also concerned with education, and provides data and statistics, information on food safety, nutritional education, and research, among others.

**Healthy Schools Health Youth!**

http://www.cdc.gov/healthyouth/

This site is aimed at establishing healthy behaviors in childhood so it will carry into adulthood. The site contains adolescent and school health tools, education resources, strategies to prevent obesity and more.

**Education World—Health Education**

http://www.educationworld.com/pe_health/health.shtml

A great web site containing physical education and health education tools, lesson plans and more.

**American School Health Association (ASHA)**

www.ashaweb.org

ASHA contributes to the health and education of children by providing school health strategies.

**Education Planet**

www.educationplanet.com

Offers resources for health and nutrition.

**Crest Kids**

http://www.crest.com/crest-kids/

Information on oral care for kids, along with an experiment to show kids the importance of brushing.

**Kraft Foods**

http://www.kraftrecipes.com/yourkids/main.aspx

Great ideas for picky eaters, lunches, dinners and lunch boxes. Also provides recipes for kids, nutrition information, and activities.

**Communities and Schools Promoting Health**

www.safehealthyschools.org

This site provides links to planning and assessment tools, lesson plans, reports, research, and more.

**SHAPE America (Society of Health and Physical Education)**

http://www.shapeamerica.org

The largest organization of professionals involved in school-based health, physical education, and physical activity. Provides resources, information, and research on physical education, physical activity along with health education, dance, early childhood education, and sport. Formally known as American Association for Health, Physical Education, Recreation, and Dance.

**Let's Move! Active Schools**

http://www.letsmoveschools.org

A part of the First Lady's Let's Move! initiative, this site helps schools develop a culture in which physical education and physical activity are foundations to academic success. Has information on resources, programs, and funding opportunities.

## Physical Activity

**SparkPE**

www.sparkpe.org

A research-based, public health organization dedicated to creating implementing and evaluating programs that promote lifelong wellness. Includes information on Physical Education, after school ideas, and coordinated school health activities.

**AYSO**

www.ayso.org

Besides getting information on the AYSO and soccer, this site also offers daily nutrition tips, and safety tips including nutrition and hydration.

**National Association for sport and Physical Education (NASPE)**

http://www.aahperd.org/naspe/

NASPE created the Let's Move in School initiative to support Michelle Obama's Let's Move campaign. Also has information on available grants, along with teaching tools and networking.

**PE 4 Life**

www.pe41ife.org

PE 4 Life believes increasing access to quality physical education will increase the activity and health of children. They work with schools in promoting this belief.

**Sports Media**

www.sports-media.org

This site contains tons of information on sports. It includes an area for educators to post lesson plans and other information to share.

**Susan's Physical Education, Health and Sports Site**

www.hccanet.org/patricks

This site was created by a PE teacher and coach for health and PE teachers and coaches. It provides classroom ideas along with resources, activities and other information.

**PE Central**

www.pecentral.org

This site offers up to date information about developmentally appropriate PE programs for kids. Also includes lesson plans, assessments, and information on adapted PE.

**PHE Canada**

www.phecanada.ca

Physical and Health education in Canada. Information on physical and health education, intramurals, and dance, along with informative articles.

**PE links 4 U**

www.pelinks4u.org

Tons of links to relevant articles, and also to PE websites for higher education and K-12, and list servs, among others.

**Awesome Library**

http://www.awesomelibrary.org/Classroom/Health_PE/Health_PE.html

This site offers information on health, nutrition, recreation and sports among other topics. It also provides lesson plans and what's new in health and physical education and research.

## Apps for PE and Health

**PE Central**

www.pecentral.com

Has a variety of apps including Teaching Games for Understanding (TGFU), tag games, and icebreaker games. Some are free, some have a fee.

**TCEA (Texas Computer Education Association)**

www.tcea.org

Free iPad apps for health and PE including a BMI Calculator, Carb Counting with Lenny, Fitness Free HD, Nexercise, and The PE Geek.

**SparkPE**

www.sparkpe.org

Includes apps for students and teachers such as Super Stretch, Yoga HD, Iron Kids, and Fitness Kids.

**Avatar**

www.avatargeneration.com

Health education apps for nutrition and fitness.

## For Kids

**Kidnetic.com**

http://www.kidnetic.com/

Great site for kids! Contains game ideas, recipes for kids, quizzes, and interactive game to learn about the human body.

**NCPAD's 14 Week Plan to a Healthier You**

http://www.ncpad.org/14weeks/

Weekly tips on how to stay motivated, workout ideas, and nutrition to help you stay on track to reach your fitness goals. Although aimed at those with disabilities, much of the information is helpful to anybody.

## Equipment

**Beacon Athletics**

http://beaconathletics.com

Among traditional equipment, also provides items that are designed for mobility and easy storage.

**Goal Sports**

www.goalsports.com

**Palos Sports**

www.palossports.com

**Flag House**

www.flaghouse.com/going-strong

Besides traditional sporting equipment, also has equipment for the special needs population.

**Kimbo Educational**

www.kinboed.com

A catalog with items related to dance, aerobics, active play including dance/exercise DVDs and special needs.

**PE Central**

www.pecentralstore.com

Includes limited space equipment, adapted equipments, activities, and many other useful items.

## Lesson Plans

**Duncan**

www.yo-yo.com/teachers.asp

Offers the opportunity to have a Duncan representative come to your school to give a demonstration, along with yo-yos for the students.

**McRel Lesson Plans**

http://www.mcrel.org/lesson-plans/health/index.asp

A collection of lesson plans organized by topic.

**Teachers Network**

http://teachernetwork.org

Lesson plans designed by teachers and organized by topic and grade level.

**HealthTeacher**

www.healthteacher.com

Provides lesson plans and also national standards.

**PE Central**

www.pecentral.org

Provides over 1800 lesson and assessment ideas submitted by other educators.

**PBS**

www.pbs.org/teachersource/helath.htm

Provides lesson plans and other resources, organized by grade level and topic.

**Awesome Library**

http://www.awesomelibrary.org/Classroom/Health_PE/Health_PE.html

This site offers information on health, nutrition, recreation and sports among other topics. It also provides lesson plans and what's new in health and physical education and research.

**The Educator's Reference Desk**

http://www.eduref.org/Virtual/Lessons/index.shtml#Search

This site contains more than 2000 lesson plans submitted by teachers from the U.S. and all over the world. Organized by topic and grade level.

**Education World**

http://www.educationworld.com/a_lesson/archives/pe.shtml

**HotChalk**

www.lessonplanspage.com

Over 4000 lesson plans available by topic and grade level. Free newsletter also available.

**LessonPlanz.com**

http://lessonplanz.com

Lesson plans organized by topic and grade level. Free newsletter available.

**teAchnology**

www.teach-nology.com

Offers over 30,000 lesson plans, along with free printable worksheets, rubrics, teaching tips and more.

**Teachnet.com**

www.teachnet.com

**Lesson Plan Central**

http://lessonplancnetral.com

Lesson plans, printable worksheet, clip art and more.

**Teachers.net**

http://physical-education.teachers.net

Provide lesson plans, chatboards, articles, projects and more.

## Music

**Best Childrens Music.com**

www.bestchildrensmusic.com

They have done the research for you, and can offer age-appropriate music of varying themes.

**Education Planet**

www.educationplanet.com

Offers resources for art and music.

**Kimbo Educational**

www.kinboed.com

A catalog with items related to dance, aerobics, active play including dance/exercise DVDs.

**PE Central**

www.pecentralstore.com

## Adapted/Special Needs

**Learning Disabilities Association of America**

www.ldanatl.org

Offers information for parents and teachers on understanding learning disabilities. Includes research, resources, and more.

## Early Childhood

**Earlychildhood.com**

www.earlychildhood.com

A resource for teacher supplies, along with activities, materials, and outcomes.

**PBS Teachers**

http://www.pbs.org/teachers/classroom/prek/health-fitness/ Broken down by grade, this site offers resources, teacher discussions, and professional development.

## Bullying

www.stopbullying.gov
Information to help stop bullying at school, online, and in the community.

**Anti-Bullying Network**

www.antibullying.net
Information for young people, parents and teachers on tackling bullying within schools.

**PACER center**

www.pacer.org
A non profit organization which provides a complete classroom tool kit for elementary school bullying prevention.

**The Trevor Project**

www.thetrevorproject.org
The leading national organization focused on suicide prevention efforts for LGBTQ youth.

## Book Resources

### General

**Teaching the Nuts and Bolts of Physical Education, 2nd Edition**
A. Vonnie Colvin, Nancy J. Egner Markos, Pamela J. Walker
©2008 ISBN 978-0-7360-6748-5
Ages 5–12
Shows mechanics & progression of basic skills.

**Developmental Physical Education for All Children, 4th Edition**
Frances Cleland Donnelly and David L. Gallahue
©2007 ISBN 978-0736071208
For future PE teachers, this book focuses on developmentally appropriate approaches and application of a variety of teaching styles. Includes six month subscription to *Journal of Teaching Pysical Education* (JTPE) and CD-ROM with lesson plans, assessments, and worksheets.
Textbook. www.amazon.com

**Health in America: A Multicultural Perspective, 3rd Edition**
M. Raymond Nakamua
©2008 ISBN 978-0-7575-5029-4
This health book is very unique in that it addresses the health issues affecting ethnic minority Americans.
Textbook, www.kendallhunt.com

**Physical Education: Tips from the Trenches**
Charmain Sutherland
©2002 ISBN 978-07-360-37098
This book details the many challenges teachers face on and off the field that you can't learn from a textbook or methods class, and how to deal with them.
www.amazon.com

**Special Physical Education, 9th Edition**
John Dunn and Carol Leitschuh
©2009 ISBN 978-0-7575-6873-2
Focuses on the best practices in adapted PE available today. Includes activities.
Textbook, www.kendallhunt.com

**Teaching Children Physical Education, 3rd Edition**
George Graham
©2009 ISBN 978-0736062106
This book presents a user-friendly view of what it takes to be a great PE teacher. Provides printable worksheets.
Textbook, www.amazon.com

**The Physical Education Teacher's Book of Lists, Teacher Edition**
Marian D. Milliken
©2002 ISBN 978-0787978877
Time-saver for new and experienced physical education teachers that provides over 250 lists related to physical education. These can be reproduced. The lists are organized in three sections: goals, games, and guides.
www.amazon.com

**Totally Awesome Strategies for Teaching Health, 7th Edition**
Linda Meeks
©2010 ISBN 978-0073404660
This books gives a variety of teaching techniques for a health class.
Textbook, www.amazon.com

### Games

**Children's Games from Around the World, 2nd Edition**
Glenn Kirchner
©2000 ISBN 978-0205296279

Provides a great way to integrate diversity in the classroom. Each game references the country of origin so children can learn about different cultures. It has two chapters explaining how to guide children to create their own games.

### Funn & Games, 1st Edition
Karl Rohnke
©2004 ISBN 978-0-7575-0846-2
If you want exciting and immediately usable ideas to implement right now, this will soon be your favorite resource.
www.kendallhunt.com

### Great Games for Young People
Marilee A. Gustafson, Sue K. Wolfe, and Cheryl L. King
©1991 ISBN 978-0-87322-299-7
A great collection of games for upper elementary through senior high school students. Descriptions and rules of the games are right to the point.
www.amazon.com

### Inclusive Games
Susan L. Kasser
©1995 ISBN 978-0-87322-639-9
This book provides activities and games for both regular and adapted PE.
www.amazon.com

### Ready—to-use PE Activities
Joanne M. Landy and Maxwell D. Landy
Series
This series of books, divided by grade level, provide ready-to-use fitness activities and games.
www.amazon.com

### Silver Bullets: A Revised Guide to Initiative Problems, Adventure Games, and Trust Activities, 2nd Edition
Karl Rohnke
©2010 ISBN 978-0-7575-6532-8
www.kendallhunt.com

## Books for Children

### Dinosaurs Alive and Well: A Guide to Good Health
Laurene Krasny
©1993 ISBN 978-0316109983
This book provides advice on nutrition, exercises, relationships, and stress relievers in simple text and illustrations.
Ages 4–8
www.amazon.com

### From Head to Toe: Big Book
Eric Carle
©2007 ISBN 978-0061119729
Encourages children to exercise by following the movements of various animals.
Ages 4–8
www.amazon.com

### Activities for the Classroom
Let's move in school
An AAHPERD website with ideas for physical activity during school, and before and after school along with ideas for physical education classes.

### Brain Breaks
www.emc.cmich.edu/BrainBreaks/
An online Physical Activity Idea Book for Elementary Classroom Teachers.

# Index